Practical Bliss

The Busy Person's Guide to Happiness

By Lisa Broesch-Weeks

http://www.PracticalBliss.com

THANK YOU!

Thank you for downloading my book.
Please be kind and REVIEW this book on Amazon. I welcome and appreciate your feedback.

To receive free bonus "Bits of Bliss" plus periodic tips designed to help you get full value from this book, click or go to the link below to subscribe:

https://in-bliss.leadpages.net/7- stress-slashers/

May you work, play, live . . . In Bliss!™

Dedicated to my husband, Larry Weeks, whose encouragement, feedback, insight, and support gave me the courage and stamina to return to Bliss.

ACKNOWLEDGEMENTS

I'm so grateful to so many who have enlightened, encouraged, and impacted my journey toward living a blissful, authentic life while doing work that brings me more joy and meaning than I could have ever imagined.

My financial advisor, attorney, and unwavering friend and supporter, Helen VonDolteren-Fournier—who was the first person to ever ask me about my dreams and has devoted herself and her expertise to helping me obtain every one of them.

My son, Kyle Broesch, whose positive attitude, sense of humor, and ability to make me proud has enabled us to create a home filled with love and laughter.

To CAPP 14 alumni and our instructor, Carin Rockind, who provided vital information, research, and enthusiastic encouragement throughout the course of my research and writing.

Marketing and author's coach, friend, and mentor, Monte Taylor, Jr., who convinced me to breathe new life into purpose-driven work and provided me with invaluable knowledge, tools, and guidance to bring this book to light.

My developmental and copy editor, Carrie White-Parrish, who helped to clarify my thoughts and made the editing process collaborative and fun.

All the experts I've mentioned throughout the book, who enthusiastically allowed me to pick their brains and glean their wisdom to support my theories.

My BlissChicks, Kim, Regena, Mary, Karen, Terese, my sister Sabrina, and too many more to list here, who have believed in and encouraged me for as long as I can remember.

The Wetherby family, who welcomed me "home" with dinner, wine, and endless laughter each month while I made the cross-country trek to complete my research.

The fun-loving, joy seeking members of our Club Bliss Community, who believe in creating a world InBliss—thank you.

Table of Contents

INTRODUCTION

"The difference between a rut and a grave is the earth above you."
—*Author Unknown*

It was September 22, 2005, and a hot, sticky, sweaty 97 degrees. In my left hand I held my ham and low-fat cheese on whole wheat bread (no mayo), and in my right I held my purse, cell phone, briefcase, car keys, and overstuffed, oversized binder. And, as if I needed something else to worry about, my dash across the pavement from my office to my 2003 Mazda Tribute to head to a meeting I had called was suddenly and irrevocably halted . . . when the right heel of my open-toe shoe got caught in the storm drain in the asphalt.

As I stood there teetering on one foot and trying to get my other heel out of the drain, my favorite employee, Melanie, ran up and started talking nonstop. She was laughing, delighted that I was a captive audience, and taking advantage of a moment to pick my brain before I rushed out to yet another meeting.

As my sandwich melted and sweat ran down the back of my dress, it occurred to me in that moment that I was *not* living in bliss.

Believe it or not, that came as a bit of a shock to me. Up until then I had been so busy dashing from meeting to meeting, scurrying to do all the things I thought I needed to do to be the success I wanted to be, that I'd hardly noticed the headaches, sleepless nights, and general exhaustion and apathy I felt on a daily basis.

To the rest of my world it probably seemed like I had it all. I was an executive with a prominent Fortune 50 company, owned a nice home, was fit and healthy, had been married for sixteen years, had money in the bank, and had a wonderful little boy at home. It should have been enough. *But it wasn't.* And at that moment, with my heel caught in the drain, the realization hit me with the subtlety of a bag of bricks.

And with it came something else: It was time to make some changes. But I felt so ashamed and alone that I didn't tell anyone how I felt. After all, I appeared to have so much more than so many others. Did I even have the *right* to want something more or something else, when so many people were working just to make ends meet? Why was I so ungrateful? What was *wrong* with me?

Soon, though, I found myself lying awake every night, trying to figure out where to start making changes. I wasn't even sure I knew what I was looking for—or if I deserved to find it. During the day, I was preoccupied with my thoughts and dreams, and growing more and more frustrated with my "perfect" little life. I knew in my heart that I wanted to slow down and stop racing to the always-elusive finish line, and add more joy, passion, and meaning to my life.

I just had no clue how to do it.

Then one day, out of the blue, a friend handed me a postcard advertising a retreat to "discover my dreams." The program promised to help me define my dreams and take immediate action. I jumped at the opportunity to fly across the country to go "find myself" and make some sense of the chaotic thoughts that regularly ran through my mind. During the retreat, I realized that for the most part I had been sleepwalking through my life (at a very fast pace). And it was time to make some big changes; I would either need to reinvigorate my marriage and career to include more purpose and passion, or create new paths for my life. That was the beginning of what has been my decade-long journey to design and create a life of bliss.

Since then, I have redesigned most everything about my life—my career, my marriage (I am now remarried), my friends, and perhaps most importantly, my relationship with myself. I also have a healthy, happy relationship with my now-teenage son, and feel immense gratitude for my new world. However, I won't say the journey has been an easy one. I made hard choices, made some monumentally *poor* decisions, and went through stages of depression and anxiety along the way. Nevertheless, I can absolutely say that it was *all worth it*—because it took me on another path, and that path led to a state of true happiness.

But it took a lot of work. And being the efficient executive I was, I got to thinking—what if there was a way to speed up the process, make better decisions, and avoid the pitfalls and anxiety along the way? What if there was a place where people who wanted to work, play, and live a "blissful" life could do so in supportive community?

What if living in bliss wasn't a destination where we expected to see rainbows and unicorns around every corner, but rather a state of mind that we naturally and purposely returned to as we went through our days?

What if we, as busy people with everyday responsibilities, could create this new and improved life **without necessarily turning our lives upside down**?

What if we could *find the time* to create and enjoy more bliss even when we traveled, worked long hours, cared for children (or parents), or were constantly on the go?

And after mulling over the idea for some time, I found my answer: *we could.*

Regardless of what your starting point may be, there *is* a way to add more purpose, engagement, and happiness to your life. Whether you want to finally take action on your lifelong dreams or simply tweak something tc make it great, you can do so—and this book will be your practical guide to taking the steps (and avoiding many of the pitfalls), and creating the life you've always wanted.

In these pages I'll share my story, as well as stories from clients, friends, and industry experts, divulge key proven secrets, and guide you toward envisioning and incorporating more of what you want into your daily life.

I'll also share practical exercises, resources, and a wealth of scientific research on how to identify what will make your life more meaningful and happy, organize your vision, and implement your plans.

By the time we're done, you'll have figured out your purpose and passion—or at least know where and how to start—mapped out a plan for finding bliss in your life, and begun connecting with the people that will keep you there.

Welcome to a safe place to create possibilities.

Welcome to Practical Bliss!

CHAPTER ONE

Not Another Airy-Fairy Self-Help Book?!

"I'd rather have 30 minutes of wonderful than a lifetime of nothing special." –Julia Roberts in Steel Magnolias

Creating everlasting happiness can be exhausting work. And we certainly never stop trying to do it.

I don't know about you, but I find myself overwhelmed by the barrage of self-help information that comes pouring into my life on a regular basis. Don't get me wrong; in the beginning of my journey, I was absolutely amazed at the resources and possibilities for helping me stretch and grow beyond my static life and long-term career. But somewhere along the way, I realized that I kept hearing the same advice from a variety of sources—much of it seeming somewhat shallow and theoretical. Where was the data and truly practical application to support the theories? *And how in the world was a person with a career, family, and responsibilities supposed to find the time?!*

It's not that I don't find personal development incredibly helpful. In fact, I hold multiple certifications in coaching for personal development, as well as a certification in applied positive psychology (the scientific study of happiness). My clients have told me time and again of the positive impact coaching has made in their lives. Yet whenever a friend or colleague introduced me as a "life coach," I was sickened by what it conjured up: images of a jack-of-all-trades, airy-fairy, rainbow skirt-wearing drifter with no experience in the professional world . . . who randomly spewed out positive affirmations and quotes from the movie, *The Secret.*[1]

Seriously, I just didn't see myself in this category. I mean, what about my twenty-plus years of corporate experience? What about my years of work as a consultant, trainer, and executive coach in the hospitality, entertainment, manufacturing, and healthcare industries? How could I—or my experience and expertise—possibly be taken seriously when I'd been introduced as a *life coach*?!

Welcome to the source of my inner turmoil. For many years, my ego and soul were in direct conflict with one another, and I couldn't for the life of me pick sides. My ego didn't think that the term would fly in the corporate world, yet my soul wouldn't let me rest.

The truth is, I found *The Secret* incredibly inspiring, and many of my friends are very gifted and successful personal development coaches (aka, life coaches) who I have learned from and respect immensely. So what *was* my issue, exactly?

At the end of the day, I realized that I saw the topics of personal development and successful professional growth as completely at odds with each other. For me, there simply wasn't enough time *or reason* for the two worlds to coexist. After all, who has time to sit around dreaming about tomorrow when there's so much to get done today?

But that was my ego talking, and my soul wouldn't take no for an answer. I just knew there was something to the idea that we could want and plan for more or different things in the

---

[1] ***The Secret*** is a 2006 film[3] produced by Prime Time Productions consisting of a series of interviews designed to demonstrate the New Thought claim that everything one wants or needs can be satisfied by believing in an outcome, repeatedly thinking about it, and maintaining positive emotional states to "attract" the desired outcome.

future . . . while simultaneously living, working, and thriving in the present.

How was I going to match those two ideas up?

And beyond that, I didn't think this was unique to me. In fact, I assumed that other people in my position would have the same question.

So I began talking with some of my friends and colleagues about the idea and definition of Living in Bliss. These conversations led me to interviews with experts in their fields (many of them in the science, technology, engineering, and medical industries), which led me to further research the benefits of creating a life that included regular doses of happiness, joy, and purpose.

What I really wanted to find out was 1) What **exactly** is bliss? and 2) **Is there a business case for it?** Are happiness and moments of bliss just a dreamy "nice to have," or are they a wise investment with an actual payoff?

So let's start with the question *what is bliss*?

For our purposes, we'll define bliss as the *point where purpose, mindfulness, and pleasure meet (*see image). In other words, "bliss" is achieved when your life has purpose, you're actively engaged with the world around you, and you incorporate pleasure into your life experiences.

Of course, your next question may be "So how do I get that??" Great question, and we'll cover that in just a bit.

First, though, let's talk about the second question: *Is there a business case for bliss?*

Throughout the course of my interviews with the experts, I was overwhelmed by the unanimously positive response to that question. Experts cited the benefits of caring for your emotional needs through regular implementation of activities that inspire thoughts and feelings of joy, hope, passion, purpose, or general well being. Those benefits ranged from better physical and mental health to anti-aging, lower stress, greater professional success, stronger families, increased physical fitness, and longer overall sustainability in both personal and professional scenarios.

In fact, *every expert I talked to* rated the importance of implementing "bliss" between a score of 9 and 10 (based on a 1-to-10 scale, with 10 being the highest rating).

Ok! Now we're talking! With all of this proof and expert opinion, my ego was finally getting on board with the idea of finding bliss and self-improvement. And I was getting excited.

The research also confirmed that I wasn't alone in my conflict between the ideas of "getting to work" and "stopping to play." The more I brought the topic up in conversation, speaking engagements, and coaching, the more I heard from other busy people who couldn't seem to stop working so hard for everyone else and start *leading lives* that were more purposeful, productive, energized, and satisfying.

Isn't it ironic that by the time you get to the point where your career has taken off, the kids are in school, and you have the house and car you wanted (or close to it), you still feel a yearning for something else . . . something missing . . . something more…?

Could it be that the elusive piece you haven't found yet is **you**??

Don't laugh, though I know it might sound ridiculous. After all, you're right here, reading this book. You're making the effort, and you're present. How could *you* be the thing missing from your otherwise picturesque life?

I get it . . . and as I mentioned earlier, I've been there myself. I'm guessing your ego is weighing in right now, probably telling you that you don't need to read any of this. After all, you've got it all! Your friends and family are envious!

That's fair. But what about that little voice inside you that longs to be heard? The piece of you that wants to dream again—to play, to rest, to have pure fun without apology? That piece of you that's asking, "**Is this all there is**? Where's the meaning in my life?"

Those are certainly great questions, and I intend to help you answer them for yourself in this book.

While it's true that not everyone has a noticeable yearning for more, you do. Am I right? In fact, you may even have asked yourself these questions in the past and thought you had them all worked out.

That's the funny thing about joy, meaning, and visions for your life: They need a "touch up" every so often, because they expand and grow as you grow. In other words, your dream or idea of meaning and happiness ten, five, or even two years ago might well have changed. And there's nothing wrong with that. In fact, as I understand it, every living thing is either in the process of growth or death. There's no middle ground here (i.e., a plant doesn't just stay at one stage—it's either in a stage of growth or death). Bearing that in mind, you as a living organism are always moving one way or the other. So which process do you choose to engage in?

There's a reason you're reading this book, and I think that gives you your answer. You've come to the conclusion that you do want more—and you're willing to listen to the reasons why that's okay. Further, you're willing to take the steps to move in that direction. I want to support you as you embark on your journey of discovery. Whether you want to do a little tune up or implement broader changes in your life, I wish to provide you with the tools, examples, research, and support to get you to your goals as quickly and practically as possible.

A word of caution here, however: The actions listed in this book may not be easily attainable by all who try. However, they are *guaranteed* to fail if they are either A) not implemented or B) predetermined to be unachievable.

One of the most difficult practices to carry out may be the act of suspending your belief. If someone had told me back in 2005 that I would change almost every aspect of my life (including both the personal and professional cornerstones I had come to depend on), I would have said, "No way! How in the world am I going to do that??"

Yet it is entirely possible to use the practical tools in this guide to design an existence that includes more of what you're searching for in your everyday life. If you believe that it can be done, and want to do it badly enough.

Your first and likely most important challenge is to focus on "what" you would like your In Bliss Life to look like, and not "how" you will make each and every change. As you begin to gain a clear picture of your design, you may be surprised to find that your outlook and actions change, and that you'll start to put yourself in situations where you draw the people, opportunities, and strategies necessary to fulfill, support, and sustain your vision. As your attitude changes, so do your actions, and you'll end up seeing opportunities where you never saw them before.

Without sitting down and hashing out exactly how it's going to happen.

One more note: Keep in mind this is not a book about creating a "perfect life." Heaven knows I'm a recovering perfectionist, and have learned that not only is it an exhausting and unachievable goal (in fact, the act of trying to be perfect is in itself imperfect); it's also a lonely road to travel. Instead, I've learned that true connection is found in our vulnerabilities, not our perfection. Our ability to admit that we're human and capable of being messy, silly, sad, hungry, anxious, and angry will help enable us to be content with who and where we are right now. In short, then, being willing to have an imperfect life—rather than keeping up with the Joneses—allows us to gain more satisfaction than a quest for absolute perfection; particularly because our idea of perfect is an ever-changing concept.

To quote Elizabeth Gilbert, author of *Eat, Pray, Love:*

The women whom I love and admire for their strength and grace did not get that way because shit worked out. They got that way because shit went wrong, and they handled it. They handled it in a thousand different ways on a thousand different days, but they handled it. Those women are my superheroes.

A perfect life, where everything works out beautifully because we planned it, is a just a mirage—one you can almost see up in the distance, but never quite reach.

In reality, life is messy and imperfect *much of the time.* And as much as we might like it to, bliss doesn't come riding in on a white horse to save you from experiencing **all** the frustration, hurt, loss, and busy-ness that comes with real life. The good news is that happiness isn't one moment or scenario in time; you can experience it in a hundred different ways, on any given day, and still be simultaneously intertwined with the messy parts of life, in order to bring you the "balanced" life we've all heard so much about.

In other words, Living in Bliss **is the difference between "making it through" another day and making every day contribute to a *life worth living!***

Yes, you can make room for happiness and meaning in your busy life, and yes you can stop feeling frivolous or guilty for wanting something more or sneaking in a little solitude, peace, and fun here and there. In fact, as you go through this book you'll find bits of information and practical exercises that will clearly show you that you can not only stop seeing bliss as an "airy-fairy" and unobtainable concept, and start looking at it as a solid investment in your long-term success, sustainability, and overall well-being.

So what are you waiting for? It's time to start investing in you!

CHAPTER TWO

The Case for Bliss (Happiness)

"Happy people sell more, are more productive, have better relationships and help other people do the same." –Alex Theis, author of Stop Pitching & Start Connecting

I think it's safe to assume that we all have our own reasons for believing we need to work as hard as we do to get where we need to go. However, how far do we think we need to go before we believe we can finally *start to enjoy* everything we've worked so hard to achieve?

Does it really have to be "all work and no play," or can we actually dare to strive for a more balanced mix of work and time to rest/play/laugh/create/enjoy/savor/and engage in our lives?

The Guilt of It All

As I mentioned earlier, one of my biggest struggles has been not in finding a few moments here and there to relax and enjoy myself, but rather not being able to fully *engage* in those moments without the bombardment of self-inflicted guilt that kept pressuring me to "Get my ass back to work!"

Maybe you can relate. For example, have you ever scheduled a couple of vacation days and then decided to go into work anyway because there were deadlines that seemed more important than taking a couple of days to rest or relax? Or have you ever actually taken a day off to be with your kids or spouse, and then wound up spending the day on the phone with employees or clients, or on your computer responding to email? One client of mine told me how she accepted a new position at work with the promise that she would have every other Friday off—which would have been great had she not decided to work those days "off" anyway so that other people wouldn't think they were working harder than she.

As I've interviewed coaching clients, workshop participants, and busy professionals from nearly every industry, the topic of guilt has come up time and time again (and again!). So I know it's not only me. In fact, I'm willing to bet that it's one of the reasons you picked up this book in the first place—that struggle between working more and harder, and taking some time to actually be happy.

We'll talk more about the guilt and self-care in the next chapter, but first I thought it might help you put your busy mind at ease to look at the "business case for bliss." After all, we're business-minded people; we want to know the logic behind the need for happiness.

Let's start with the purely business-related research about the benefits of bliss. According to Alex Theis, author of the bestselling book *Stop Pitching & Start Connecting*[2]:

How you feel, your attitude, how you start and go about your day—it all reflects on how you deal with people and your business dealings.

---

[2] Alex is the author of the Amazon bestselling book *Stop Pitching & Start Connecting*, a social media guide for entrepreneurs and home-based business people. His podcast is called Limitless, and focuses on helping people see that they can break through limits and obstacles. Alex can be contacted at Alextheis.com and podcastlimitless.com hipcast.com @alextheis.

*At the end of the day it's all about relationships. If you're in your zone, smiling and having a good time, you're **responding instead of reacting**. Customers, clients, business dealings are all going to reflect that back to you.*

In fact, research by Lyubomirsky, King and Diener (2005) shows that "happiness correlates with a robust number of positive life outcomes."[3]

At work, happy and satisfied people are more likely to:

- Secure more job interviews
- Find work with more autonomy, meaning, and variety
- Take fewer sick days
- Experience less "burnout"
- Think more creatively and flexibly at work[4]
- Have more positive evaluations from supervisors and customers
- Have superior performance and productivity
- Optimists have more success in sales positions[5]
- Handle managerial positions better
- Even as CEOs, receive higher performance ratings and head companies with greater return on investment[6]
- As companies, have happier employees who produce more, and are more profitable[7]

---

[3] Lyubomirsky, Sonja, Laura King, and Ed Diener. "The benefits of frequent positive affect: does happiness lead to success?." *Psychological Bulletin* 131.6 (2005): 803.
[4] Boehm, Julia K, and Sonja Lyubomirsky. "Does happiness promote career success?" *Journal of Career Assessment* 16.1 (2008): 101-116.
[5] "Seligman SASQ (Optimism / Resilience) Profiling, Foresight," 2008, http://www.foresight.co.nz/index.asp?pageID=2145821038 (accessed April 15, 2016).
[6] "The Business Case—Silver Lining Psychology," 2013, http://www.silverliningpsychology.com/what-we-do/the-business-case/ (accessed January 5, 2016).

- Be relatively more successful in the workplace[8]

I spoke with a technical solutions manager with Google, who also holds a Ph.D. in theoretical physics, who had this to say about the business case for bliss:

Bliss is about engaging in what makes you happy. It may not be quantifiable, it's more intangible, but you can't let go of the idea that being happy is more important than anything else in your life. I give bliss a 10; historically I've ignored what I need to make me happy. I think that being happier has driven more career success for me.

For most of us, it's critical to focus on being happy outside of work, or we'll risk not being as effective at work. But he also states that the challenge to be happy doesn't stop with your efforts at home. He said that Google, the #1 company to work for,[9] is known for its dedication to creating positive work environments and experiences—which goes a long way toward creating happiness at work (and home), and results in better overall performance, creativity, and productivity. Essentially, companies that run in more positive ways create happier employees, which leads to better results at home and at work.

One of the beautiful things about working for Google is that they reinforce that you're a valuable human being by providing fun perks. Even if you don't take advantage of it, it's a wonderful feeling to have the opportunity to be part of an organization where they think that you deserve that . . . It's kind of a social experience—you want

---

[7] Forbes, "Happy Employees = Hefty Profits," 2014, http://www.forbes.com/sites/meghanbiro/2014/01/19/happy-employees-hefty-profits/ (accessed January 5, 2016).
[8] Boehm, Julia K, and Sonja Lyubomirsky. "Does happiness promote career success?." *Journal of Career Assessment* 16.1 (2008): 101-116.
[9] According to Fortune.com.

*to feel part of a community that values you . . . it's not so much the tangible things, it's also the organizational things, that people take good care of you and that your boss cares whether or not you're happy—and that's been very important to my success in that organization . . . the trust that you're given to express and do things you think are right is huge, and combined together makes happier people—and **happier people are going to make better decisions for the company.***

In other words, Google actively helps its employees seek bliss through the work environment, which in turn keeps the employees happier outside of work. That ease within the workplace turns into ease outside of the workplace, and transitions into bliss in life. Google has the right idea. But what do you do if you don't work for Google, and don't work in a environment that takes your personal happiness into account?

Business and Bliss

Google isn't the only entity to notice this. When it comes to the business case for bliss, studies show that people perform better when they're happier.[10] Further, it's important to keep in mind that perks are only a small part of the happiness equation. In fact, there are many components that work together to help create a more positive environment for employees and their leaders. It's entirely possible to create a more productive, creative, and engaged organization, particularly if you're the leader, just by adopting a more positive and engaged environment!

---

[10] "Debate: Employee Happiness Matters More Than You Think," 2012, http://www.businessweek.com/debateroom/archives/2012/02/employee_happiness _matters_more_than_you_think.html (accessed January 6, 2016).

According to Teresa Amabile and Steven Kramer, authors of *The Progress Principle:*[11]

People are more productive and creative when they have more positive emotions. In fact, we found that, if happier on a given day, people were not only more likely to come up with a new idea or solve a complex problem that same day, but also to do so the next day.

Amabile and Kramer also note:

Gallup quantified the link between employee feelings and corporate outcomes, reporting that lost productivity due to employee disengagement costs more than $300 billion in the U.S. annually. A separate Gallup study by researcher James Harter and his colleagues found that business unit sales and profits at one point in time are predicted by employees' feelings about the organization at earlier points in time.

That "positive, engaged environment" includes adopting positive organizational behaviors in the workplace, such as:[12]

—**Job variety**: Provide opportunities for employees to experience other skills and roles to create variety and engagement.
—**Intrinsic motivation**: Allow employees flexible schedules, opportunities to network, and resources for professional development.
—**Confidence:** Consistently recognize employee expertise and build self-efficacy and confidence.

---

[11] Amabile, Teresa, and Steven Kramer. *The Progress Principle: Using Small Wins to Ignite Joy, Engagement, and Creativity at Work*. Brighton, MA: Harvard Business Press, 2011.
[12] Henry, J. "Positive and Creative Organization—Positive Psychology in ..." 2012, http://onlinelibrary.wiley.com/doi/10.1002/9780470939338.ch17/summary.

—**Creativity**: Allow opportunities and encourage creative thinking.

—**Team Building**: Create opportunities to build teams throughout the organization through workshops, retreats, and exercises, and support the team's initiatives.

—**Flow**: Allow opportunities to match employee interests and skills by providing clear goals and timely feedback.

—**Open climate, empowerment, and self-organization:** Allow employees to manage their own teams and invest in the company.

—**Strength work and metaperspective**: Create a greater focus on building employee strengths rather than singular focus on weakness (Gallup research has found that "If your supervisor focuses on your strengths, your chances of actively disengaging at work are only one in one hundred."[13])

With that in mind, it's important to remember as well that if you're the leader, your happiness (or lack thereof) can significantly impact your ability to create the essential elements of happy environments. That means that you must take care of yourself first if you're to take care of anyone else. Roberta Matuson,[14] author of bestselling books *Suddenly In Charge* and *Talent Magnetism*, puts it like this:

As the leader, when you deprive yourself of bliss, it can have an impact on your patience and understanding . . . Executives often find a million reasons why they can't slow down or have bliss . . .

---

[13] "Driving Engagement by Focusing on Strengths—Gallup," 2014, http://www.gallup.com/businessjournal/124214/driving-engagement-focusing-strengths.aspx (accessed April 15, 2016).

[14] Roberta Matuson is president of Matuson Consulting and author of *Talent Magnetism: How to Build a Workplace That Attracts and Keeps the Best* as well as the bestselling author of *Suddenly in Charge: Managing Up, Managing Down, Succeeding All Around.* www.Matusonconsulting.com

Step back and look at what's important and try to move a few things forward a mile rather than a bunch of things forward an inch.

Obviously, in order to maintain *your* ability to keep your cool under pressure, and spread your joy throughout the organization, you're going to need to build your reserves! Not to worry—you're headed in the right direction. And the return on your efforts to build your own happiness extends to more than just the business side.

In fact, when I interviewed Dr. Terese Roth, emergency medicine physician and fellow of the American College of Emergency Physicians, she had this to say about the business benefits of "bliss":

It's critically important to maintain a balance in your personal and professional life so that you can care for those who depend on you. When you're a person who's in a high-pressure environment or career, it's essential to keep yourself grounded so that you can calmly do what needs to be done while putting others at ease . . . When you're going through the motions and rushing through your life, trying to do too many things at once, you're not really paying attention, and you can make mistakes which contribute to car and kitchen accidents, home- and work-related injuries, and more.

All that is to say, whether you're an entrepreneur, CEO, manager, or individual contributor, your success in business is impacted significantly by your overall happiness and well-being. This is a two-way street; companies and employees are dependent on each other when it comes to happiness. Employees depend on leaders to set the tone and create the circumstances for positive environments, and companies gain better results from happy employees. When employees work for a happier, more successful company, it contributes to creating a happier life. In other words, everyone's happy.

Beyond the Bottom Line

Research shows that you can benefit from happiness in virtually *every area of your life.*

In Relationships,[15] happy people are more likely to:

- Have friends they can rely on (and having friends has the highest positive correlation with happiness)[16]
- Be more satisfied with their friends
- Be more satisfied with social activities
- Be less jealous of others
- Report less loneliness
- Have more satisfying social relationships
- Have more fulfilling marriages
- Describe their romantic partners as their "great love"

In Health and Personal areas,[17] happy people are more likely to:

- Take less medication
- Have fewer hospital visits
- Have stronger immune systems
- Report fewer physical symptoms
- Report less substance abuse
- Have fewer visits to the emergency room[18]

---

[15] Diener, Ed, and Martin EP Seligman. "Very happy people." *Psychological Science* 13.1 (2002): 81-84.
[16] Friedman, Howard, and Leslie R Martin. *The longevity project: surprising discoveries for health and long life from the landmark eight decade study.* Hay House, Inc, 2011.
[17] Lyubomirsky, Sonja, Laura King, and Ed Diener. "The benefits of frequent positive affect: does happiness lead to success?." *Psychological Bulletin* 131.6 (2005): 803-855.

- Have more favorable perceptions of themselves and others

Dr. Roth also notes that:

When people don't create natural bliss in their lives, they can make poor decisions such as drinking to excess, drug overdose, overeating . . . trying to create sort of an artificial bliss, and resulting in more trips to the emergency room.

Bliss and Your Brain

When it comes to the benefits of bliss on your brain, Dr. Daniel Thomas, an anti-aging physician,[19] had this to say:

If you want to live a longer, healthier life, studies show that people who implement bliss and take action to improve their health by spending time in nature or with friends, can have better brain health and a host of other health benefits . . . When you start taking care of your "bliss" it helps you to get in a positive mental attitude that can contribute to a desire to take better care of yourself, which can lead to overall better health.

It's important to also note that the more we learn about how to grow and apply positivity in our lives, the more we can create bonds and control how our brain responds to "fight or flight" situations—which helps us manage our response to the everyday stressors in our lives.

As John Medina, author of *Brain Rules*[20] states, "The brain wasn't designed for long-term stress, it was designed for short threats like escaping a dinosaur."

---

[18] According to Dr. Terese Roth, emergency medicine physician and fellow of the American college of emergency physicians.
[19] Dr. Daniel Thomas is an anti-aging physician, with over twenty-five years of experience, and is passionate about helping his patients live healthier, happier, and longer lives.www.HealthyandStrong.com.

Bill Cortright, author of *The NEW Stress Response Diet and Lifestyle Program*, and international professional speaker, agrees, and adds:

> When you're operating in a *"fight or flight"* mode (Mammalian brain/limbic system), it shuts down all aspects of wellness and sets us up to sabotage ourselves towards personal growth . . . Stress is not really bad, and it's not really good. It's just a response . . . it can never be shut off, it can just be managed . . . stress affects every single thing that happens in the body, from our weight to our memory, our wellness and energy . . . even to procrastination.[21]

Bill also states that one of the first ways to manage our response to stress is through our diet and the ways in which we add movement (exercise) to our day. In other words, bliss affects more than just our minds.

Happy, Healthy, and Fit?

It turns out, too, that when we invest in our self-care, including our bliss, we set ourselves up for healthier weight and fitness levels, and perhaps even a healthier response to stress.

Leslie Davis,[22] founder and CEO of FITSSIMPLE, certified fitness instructor, and an elite Team Beachbody® Coach, believes that happiness can have a profound impact on our ability to get (and stay) physically fit.

---

[20] " Medina, John. "Brain Rules: Brain development for parents, teachers and..." 2007, http://www.brainrules.net/ (accessed April 15, 2016).
[21] Bill Cortright - Author of *The Five Links to Permanent Weight Loss, The 30 Days to Change, The Ten Minute Life Plan,* and *The NEW Stress Response Diet and Lifestyle Program* http://billcortright.com/.
[22] Leslie is the founder and CEO of FITSSIMPLE. She's a certified fitness instructor and a top Team Beachbody coach http://fitssimple.com/.

When you deprive yourself of your emotional needs/bliss—you start to break down mentally and physically . . . increased stress, unhappiness, resentment, fatigue—all can lead to overeating, weight gain, tying emotion to food, and loss of motivation. When you take that dip you've got to take inventory of yourself and understand what might be out of balance so you can correct it. It's vital to your overall health and fitness.

Not to worry—we'll talk more specifically about *how* to add more bliss and manage stress throughout the book.

For now, it's important to establish **why adding more bliss to your life extends benefits to every aspect of your life.**

In fact, The Men of the Harvard Grant Study, a seventy-five-year study to discover what makes men happy, and the results of that happiness, is summarized by Robert Waldinger (current director of the Study of Adult Development)[23] as this: **High-quality, positive relationships (rather than money and fame) help us live longer, healthier, and happier lives.**

As you can see, the case for bliss yields an incredibly solid return on your investment. Now that we've gotten that out of the way, you can tell that little voice of guilt to go have a seat, because when it comes to bliss, you can't afford *not* to invest your time and energy. In fact, you might even enjoy it!

---

[23] "What makes a good life? Lessons from the longest study on ..." 2015, http://www.ted.com/talks/robert_waldinger_what_makes_a_good_life_lessons_fro m_the_longest_study_on_happiness?language=en (accessed January 6, 2016).

CHAPTER THREE

Well Now You're Just Being Self-Centered

"If you are in bliss when you give of yourself, then you are in integrity. If you need boundaries but don't use them, you're not."
–Mother Theresa

"Ok, bite down . . . now tap, tap, tap . . . good . . . How does that feel? Any better? Don't worry, we're almost there."

I could hear them talking as I sat reclined in the chair, contentedly inhaling nitrous oxide, and feeling appreciative about my dentist and her assistant's attention to detail and concern for my comfort. They went on chatting as they worked.

Dr. Torres: "I need to make a dish to bring to my dad's house tonight."

Hygienist: "What are you making?"

Dr. Torres: "Oh, just a broccoli casserole."

Hygienist: "I love making broccoli casserole! Are you adding chicken? Almonds?"

Dr. Torres: "Um, no. I've never made it before. Just some broccoli . . . and some cheese. . . I think . . ."

I heard Dr. Torres' voice trail off, and suddenly grow tense. Was that doubt I heard? Was it possible that this young woman and mother, who had been nothing short of outstanding in the care and quality of work that she'd provided me (did I mention that I had so many crowns in my mouth that

I should be queen, and that I was deathly afraid of any type of dental work?), may have entered that whirly swirly place of guilt and shame because she didn't have the perfect recipe or expertise to whip up a culinary masterpiece after the end of her work day?

Yes, it's possible that I may have been projecting. Or maybe not. The truth is, in my experience with so many of my clients (male and female alike), I've found that we almost all have a tendency to want to exceed expectations in *every* area of our lives. It's not enough to take care of our kids (or parents) or friends or family . . . or skyrocket in our careers . . . or volunteer and say "Yes" to whatever comes our way . . . or help our co-workers . . . or create a beautiful home life . . . or give and give until we give ourselves away!

Let's face it: In the U.S., it seems the trend is to be over extended, underappreciated, and basically worn to a frazzle. If we're not, then perhaps we're just not working hard enough.

Ok, I get it. I've fallen into that trap of perfection more than once in my life, often for years (or decades)! But how long can we sustain that kind of stress and strain without our wells running dry? As I mentioned in the previous chapter, our brains and bodies simply weren't designed for long-term stress and exertion. We don't ask our vehicles to run nonstop without adding fuel and oil, so why do we expect ourselves to run and run without adding the essential elements to re-energize our body, mind, and spirit? As we saw in the previous chapter, we need to make sure that our bodies have the right upkeep, through happiness and lack of stress, so that we can keep going, and going *well*.

Somewhere along the line, though, it seems to have become widely acceptable, even highly *respected*, to be as selfless as possible, at the expense of our own health. This leads, in turn, to a lack of self-care, and a general lack of

Living in Bliss. And it seems selfless—like we're working so hard to take care of others.

So essentially, we're selling out on the chance of achieving bliss for ourselves, all to help others—and we're not helping anyone in the process. We have to get out of that mindset if we're going to move forward to Living in Bliss and truly helping those around us. But how do we do it?

The question is, at what point does that so-called selfless behavior actually become *selfish*? When do we say that we may be doing it for the wrong reasons, or that we're doing it to impress other people and make them like and value us more? And when do we admit that it's not doing anyone any good—least of all us? At some point we're going to crash land without any warning to those who depend on us, and leave them standing high and dry. If you ask me, *that's* pretty selfish!

And it's certainly not a way to be living with any bliss.

But how did you get there? After all, you're the one who consistently said "Yes" where you should've said "No." And at the end of the day, it's your job to stop doing that—your job to take care of both yourself and those depending on you. It's not like anyone else is going to say to you, "Listen, I know you've been so awesome at providing for my every need and being there whenever I've needed you. Could you just stop doing that?" No, that's never going to happen. And that's where the conflict comes in.

A conflict that we've created for ourselves.

In fact, in my experience teaching conflict resolution workshops to thousands of people in a vast array of industries (from neurosurgeons to coal miners) across the United States, my participants have confirmed that one of the top causes of conflict is the resentment we often feel when we're delivering on an agreement that we never should have said "Yes" to in the first place. Because we're always fighting a two-pronged battle: the battle of knowing what we can and can't or should and shouldn't do, versus the inclination to try to be everything to everyone.

Don't get me wrong. *I'm absolutely not saying* that we shouldn't volunteer or commit ourselves to caring for or supporting others. But, it's important to make sure that when you are selfless, it's for the right reasons. For example, if your purpose[24] is to show compassion, you're probably actually *energized* when you volunteer for that sort of thing! In fact, research shows that giving our time, money, or other gifts (up to a certain point), enhances the level of well being in our lives.[25] However, if you're constantly giving, to the detriment of yourself and/or your family, for extended periods of time, you're likely at risk of actually *diminishing* your well being.

And your well being is a big part of living a purposeful, engaged, and pleasurable life.

The What and How of Well Being

So what does "well being" really mean, and how do we create and maintain it in our lives?

That's a question I tossed around for the last decade, until I came across The Foresight Report, conducted by the New Economics Foundation,[26] which reviewed over four hundred pieces of well being scientific research from around

---

[24]Note, we'll talk more about finding your purpose in Chapter 4.
[25]Diener, Edward, and Shigehiro Oishi. "Money and happiness: Income and subjective well-being across nations." *Culture and Subjective Well-Being* (2000): 185-218.
[26] "Five Ways to Wellbeing: The Evidence | New Economics ..." 2013, http://www.neweconomics.org/publications/entry/five-ways-to-well-being-the-evidence (accessed April 15, 2016).

the world (2008). The report suggests five consistent findings of activities that will increase our wellbeing:

1. **Connecting to others**—Identify the relationships most important to you and invest time and energy into building those relationships.
2. **Staying active**—Take care of the body and the mind.
3. **Savoring**—Literally stopping to smell the roses (more on this later).
4. **Continuous learning**—Engage your mind.
5. **Giving**—Commit random acts of kindness.

Ok, that doesn't sound so hard. In fact, it's important to note that *all five activities* are within our control, don't necessarily cost a cent, and can be accomplished on a weekly, if not daily, basis.

When looking at elements that may be *outside* of our immediate control, the Gallup Organization's data, which includes qualitative and quantitative inquiries, also states that there are five essential elements for well being: Career, Social, Financial, Physical, and Community.[27] The research also indicates that we'll feel out of balance if we don't focus on all five elements. Unfortunately, the research also reveals that while 66 percent of us are doing well in at least one of these areas, only 7 percent report doing well in all five areas![28]

Well, no wonder we feel out of alignment or like we haven't yet achieved the much sought-after "balance" in our lives! There's a heck of a lot to consistently focus on! And take

---

[27] Rath, T. "The Economics of Wellbeing," 2015, http://www.wtamu.edu/webres/File/Student%20Support/Career%20Services/StrengthsQuest/The_Economics_of_Wellbeing.pdf.

[28] "The Five Essential Elements of Wellbeing—Gallup," 2014, http://www.gallup.com/businessjournal/126884/five-essential-elements-wellbeing.aspx (accessed April 15, 2016).

note of the fact that doing things for others is only one of the five important actions. Which means overpromising (and under performing) is doing more damage than good, in terms of our bliss.

Want to measure your well being? Check out Gallup Inc.'s Wellbeing Finder™ here: http://www.wbfinder.com/content/126341/program.aspx.

One super-quick way to get a sense of your overall state of well being is to use the "Ladder of Life,"[29] which taps into present and future happiness.

Try this:

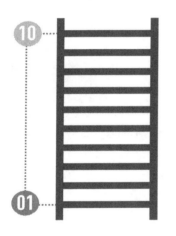

Imagine that the top of the ladder (the tenth step) is your best possible life, and the bottom (first step) is worst. First, identify which step of the ladder you'd say you stand on right now. Now identify which step you believe you'll stand on five years from now. Have you got your scores in mind? Let's take a look at the results.

[29] "Cantril Self-Anchoring Striving Scale—Gallup," 2009, http://www.gallup.com/poll/122453/understanding-gallup-uses-cantril-scale.aspx (accessed April 15, 2016).

Scoring:[30]

Depending on which step of the ladder you choose as your current step, and which you foresee as your step five years from now, you will likely fall into one of the three categories below.

Thriving: "Wellbeing that is strong, consistent, and progressing. These respondents have positive views of their present life situation (step 7+) and have positive views of the next five years (step 8+). They report significantly fewer health problems, fewer sick days, less worry, stress, sadness, anger, and more happiness, enjoyment, interest, and respect."

Struggling: "Wellbeing that is moderate or inconsistent. These respondents have moderate views of their present life situation (step 5 to 6) OR moderate OR negative views of their future. They are either struggling in the present, or expect to struggle in the future. They report more daily stress and worry about money than the 'thriving' respondents, and more than double the amount of sick days. They are more likely to smoke, and are less likely to eat healthy."

Suffering: "Wellbeing that is at high risk. These respondents have poor ratings of their current life situation (step 4 and below) AND negative views of the next five years (step 4 and below). They are more likely to report lacking the basics of food and shelter, more likely to have physical pain, a lot of stress, worry, sadness, and anger. They have less access to

---

[30] "Understanding How Gallup Uses the Cantril Scale," 2009, http://www.gallup.com/poll/122453/understanding-gallup-uses-cantril-scale.aspx (accessed April 15, 2016).

health insurance and care, and more than double the disease burden, in comparison to "thriving" respondents."

So where did you land on the ladder? Would you say the results sound pretty accurate?

You might be asking what this has to do with bliss. The point is not to judge ourselves as being above or below average, but to identify where we are now and how we can continue to build and maintain our level of well being so that we consistently fall on steps 7 and above on the ladder. We shouldn't be comparing ourselves to others, or engaging in the rat race here. We should be figuring out how we feel about where *we* are right now, and where we're going. As we progress through the book, I'll share specific interventions you can do to help yourself reach and maintain your goals.

The Tape Measure

"Keep your tape measure to yourself."—Regena Garrepy[31]

Speaking of judging ourselves, this seems like a good time to go back to that idea that creating more bliss in your life isn't about creating a *perfect* life. By no means do we need to wait until everything in our lives is buttoned up and perfect before deciding we've earned the right to start allowing ourselves the benefit of care for our own body, mind, and spirit. This is something we can start doing today, and keep doing every day from here on out,

---

[31] Regena Garrepy empowers women to unmask their essence, unveil their power and truly become the leaders of their lives without guilt or apology. She also serves as the training director for TUT.com and author Mike Dooley from Notes From the Universe. RegenaGarrepy.com

I can't tell you how many times a client has said to me, "I just need to get everything worked out and under control before I can start to work on my own stuff." But what happens then is that we're so focused on fixing everything and creating *future* bliss that we miss out on the joy and peace that's in front of us *right now*. As I've mentioned earlier, it's entirely possible to experience joy, meaning, and happiness in the midst of less-than-perfect conditions (just as it's entirely possible to love someone even though you might not *like* them every minute of every day). But we have to find a way to do that. Wishing for it won't make it happen—we have to take action.

Which is exactly why you've picked up this book.

Now that you have your score from above, what are you going to do about it? Are you ready to increase your bliss, and put a plan into action for improving your well being? Then keep reading! We're going to move through a couple more points of proof, and then we're going to jump into the things you can do immediately to climb that ladder.

Another trap to avoid is what my dear friend, Regena Garrepy, calls the "Shitty List of Shoulds." Meaning, when we start looking at what everyone else believes we "should be" or "should do" in order to qualify as a success, we relinquish our ability to self-monitor our progress. This goes back to what I've said before about doing things to impress others, or to build our reputation. It's not making us happy, and it's not actually leading us to bliss. In fact, it's putting more pressure on us than we need! But how do we *stop*?

As Regena puts it:

When we constantly look outside ourselves to see how we measure up to everyone else, we stay outside ourselves and feel disconnected to our confidence and power. We're all on our own *journey and need to trust ourselves rather than think we **should be** this or that.*

If you're really looking to challenge yourself, be brave enough to create and stick to the boundaries **you** feel you need, so that you're able to allow space and time to care for yourself and your priorities. Don't adhere to what other people think you should be doing. Decide for yourself what will make you happy, and then build a plan for how to achieve it. We'll be going over how to build that plan in the next few chapters. In the meantime, let's look at your current level of satisfaction in all areas of life, using only your honest-to-goodness standards (and no one else's).

Try This:

Look at each area of your life as represented in the Wheel of Life Inventory and shade in your satisfaction level in each of those areas of your life. Note that areas closest to the center indicate lower satisfaction and areas furthest from the center indicate higher satisfaction levels. **A word of caution here:** This information is for your use only, and will help you develop a "baseline" indicator of your own measurement for how satisfied you are in each area of your life.

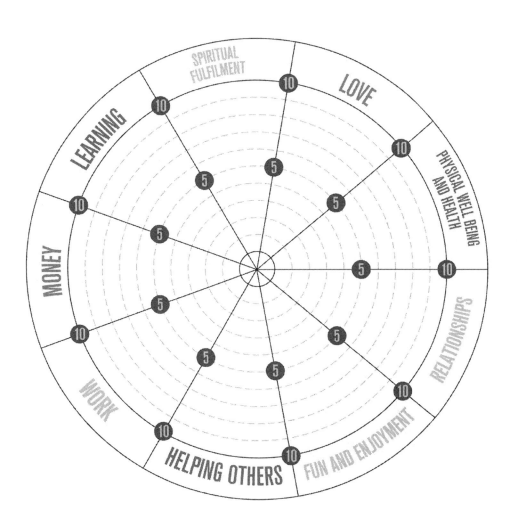

Self-Care without Self-Compassion=Self Condemnation

I'd be doing a disservice to everyone if I didn't pause for a moment to talk about the importance of not only self-care, but also *self-compassion.* And this is the perfect place to do it, because we're already talking about how to improve your well being . . . which starts with caring for yourself. For years now, I've known how incredibly important it is for us to include our own needs in the equation. However, I will be the first to say that knowing it and doing it wasn't always without a certain amount of guilt! I can't tell you how many times I'd be sitting and staring at an incredible sunrise or practicing yoga or meditation while *at the **same time*** internally beating myself up because I had the nerve to spend time watching the sunrise while others were dashing off to work. Talk about lazy! Yes, I was the master of self-condemnation.

Which is the exact opposite of self-care, and leads you down the wrong road, if your goal is bliss.

And I'm not the only one who realizes this. TED Talk speaker and one of the leading experts on self-compassion, Dr. Kristin Neff,[32] has grounded her work in the necessity of extending ourselves "the same type of kindness and care we would extend to a good friend."

Without question, though, I can honestly say that the idea of self-compassion hadn't occurred to me before. I spent so much time trying to do things and take care of everyone around me that I honestly never thought about what I was doing to my own body—or that I should be taking care of myself as well. But once I gained that step, it changed everything. Now, it shapes the way I view and regulate my internal dialogue. And that's never going to change. Because

---

[32] "Self-Compassion." 2007. 26 Apr. 2016 <http://self-compassion.org/

if we want to truly live in bliss—and take care of those we love—then we have to start by taking care of ourselves.

In her TED Talk,[33] Dr. Neff shares the belief that when we try to hold ourselves to unrealistic expectations, we set ourselves up for failure:

... We feel abnormal when we're not perfect. That separates us from others and lowers our self worth and raises our self-criticism . . . self-criticism undermines our self-motivation and attacks our self-concept. In response it releases cortisol, increases stress, and induces depression.

That sounds about right. Are you recognizing your own progression in this, too? I know that anytime I've decided to give myself a good ass kicking, it typically leads to more stress and anxiety, if not depression. None of which made my life any better. In fact, it made my sense of well being even *worse*.

On the flip side, Dr. Neff shares that "When we praise ourselves and give ourselves compassion, we release endorphins and create motivation." She goes on to talk about the physical and emotional benefits of comforting yourself, even giving yourself a hug, when you are in situations where you simply can't control the outcome.

Think about it: When's the last time you gave yourself praise for meeting a deadline, following through on goals, taking care of your children, coming up with a good idea, or simply showing up when you'd rather stay in bed? I'll bet your life is filled with responsibilities you've maintained for so long now that you automatically take care of them without ever thinking to acknowledge your successful efforts. Where's the self-compassion in that?

---

[33] Dr. Kristin Neff, "The Space Between Self-Esteem and Self Compassion..." 2013, http://tedxtalks.ted.com/video/The-Space-Between-Self-Esteem-a (accessed April 15, 2016).

To effectively measure your self-compassion, try out Dr.Neff's test at http://self-compassion.org/test-how-self-compassionate-you-are/. Your ability to nurture and truly appreciate yourself for who you are goes a long way toward boosting your resilience and helping you bounce back more quickly in times of stress, hurt, and loss. Seeing where you excel and where you need help in that process will help you when it comes to building a plan to take yourself into more blissful living.

Beauty and the Beast

Some time ago, I decided it was time to tame my tropical (and **very** overgrown) back yard. I had a vision of unearthing the potential I knew it had, and I was on a mission. In this intense labor of love, I spent more than seventy-five hours hand pulling weeds, trimming palm trees, cleaning my wooden fence, and re-staining my pool deck. I had almost conquered the jungle and felt incredibly satisfied, but there was one thing left to do: cut down the massive fourteen-foot hibiscus tree that was taking over a good part of my (and my neighbor's) yard. You see, I always hated hibiscus. I know— how can anybody hate hibiscus? I can't explain, though—I just did. A lot. So I set off to chop it down and kill it.

So I'm out there, lopping off branches and sawing off parts of the trunk (I even had to get a chainsaw involved), and as I chopped away at the branches, I tossed each one into a pile. When I eventually cut off the final limb, I turned to look at the enormous pile and noticed ... hey, those flowers are . . . pretty. Suddenly, out of nowhere, my sense of accomplishment turned to guilt and remorse. I felt terrible about cutting the tree down to nothing. How could I have purposely stripped away something so beautiful, without even realizing what I was doing?

I quickly snipped the flowers off the branches and gathered them into a vase. When I stepped back to admire them, I was so moved that I actually started to tear up with emotion. The flowers were so beautiful; and to think, I almost threw them out with the *trash*.[34]

I suddenly wondered how many times I had done that to myself over the years. How many times have we all done this to ourselves? How many times have I chopped away at the gifts and beauty I've been given, never really understanding why, just continuously (figuratively) hacking away at the parts of myself that I felt weren't good enough? Never truly appreciating the extensions of my personality, strengths, and talents that have been right in front of me the whole time.

Sound familiar?

That day, I vowed to myself that I would consciously choose to find the inner and outer beauty in myself and others, rather than wasting time cutting myself down. I won't lie—the temptation is usually there, and I still hear from my "inner critic" on occasion. When I do, I remind myself of something one of my coaches told me: "Integrity means that you're in the right relationship with **yourself**." I have always loved that saying, as it grounds me and reminds me to listen to my inner wisdom. If I "hear" something that is useful in building myself up, I take heed. Otherwise, I shut it down. I encourage you to do the same; don't wait until it's too late to turn back and appreciate what you've had all along. You can start right now, in this moment, to notice and appreciate all that is beautiful in you. Beauty comes in so many forms, both inside and out, and

---

[34] I felt so moved, I planted another hibiscus in its place and have since added two more bushes. I think hibiscuses are now one of my favorite flowers!

recognizing where your beauty lies is the first step toward creating and culminating self-compassion and ultimately bliss.

Remember, not only is it OK to love and take care of yourself; it's essential to your overall well being. So let's see where you may have some room to expand your self-care and self-compassion.

Exercise – Giving Yourself Away?

In what areas are you "giving" to the detriment of yourself/your family? On the lines below, list some examples of tasks or commitments that you could say "No" to because they are doing you and your family more harm than good. Example: I say "Yes" to every favor that's asked of me, hoping that I will be loved/valued more as a result. Or, I constantly volunteer to be on committees or projects (that I'm not really interested in) because I'm afraid no one else will step up.

_____

_____

_____

_____

In what areas do you feel your "inner critic" may be excessive? On the lines below, write down some examples of where and how self-criticizing may be harming you. Example: I find myself constantly comparing myself (personally and professionally) to others and it's hurting my self-esteem. Or, if I worked every spare moment, I'd be respected by the people I'm trying to impress.

_____

_____

_____

_____

_____

_____

What habits or thoughts can you eliminate (or begin) to improve your self-compassion and care, starting now? On the lines below, write down your answers. Example: I can limit my volunteering to **only** those projects that I truly feel passionate about. Or, I resolve to build myself and others up, rather than knocking myself down, by looking for what I love and appreciate about myself and others and eliminating the tendency to hone in on "imperfections."

_____

_____

_____

_____

_____

You are important to those who directly (and indirectly) count on you every day. And, as Dr. Neff says, "When we keep our heart open to ourselves, we keep it open to others." When you focus on self-centering and self-compassion, you're ensuring that you are able to sustain your ability to be there for those who count on you. I really can't think of anything more selfless than that.

And when you feel that you're truly serving others, while nourishing your soul, you are definitely on the path to creating the blissful, sustainable life you long for.

CHAPTER FOUR

Target Practice in the Dark

"He who has a why to live for can bear with almost any how."
—German Philosopher, Friedrich Nietzsche[35]

As I've previously mentioned, bliss is found at the intersection where a purposeful, engaged life meets with pleasure. Now that we've sorted out what may or may not be taking you down the wrong path in life, we're going to tackle what you can do to get on the *right* path so that you can more easily ensure that you will arrive at that blissful intersection. In this chapter we're going to dig into a topic that's been in mainstream discussion quite a bit in the last decade or two (and around *far* longer than that!)—purpose. Purpose is the basis for a blissful, meaningful life, and can yield quite a return when you invest a little time and effort into uncovering what your personal purpose may be. That being said, if you only read one chapter in this book, this is the topic that can really help set you on your path to bliss. So let's get started!

Purpose Can Be Found in the Most Unlikely Places

---

[35]"Friedrich Nietzsche (Stanford Encyclopedia of Philosophy),"
http://plato.stanford.edu/entries/nietzsche/ (accessed March 2, 2016).

As I write this, I'm reminded of a time when I was in an airport, hurrying to catch a connecting flight. As I dashed into the restroom (or tried to dash—there was quite a long line), I couldn't help but notice a woman who was walking around the restrooms, smiling and singing at the top of her lungs. I mean, the **top of her lungs.** I have to be honest; at first it was a little irritating. Being serenaded through the stall door, while using the restroom, isn't as uplifting an experience as you might imagine. However, by the time I had stepped to the sink, looked around, and noticed all of the women around me smiling and giving this gospel girl a high-five as they left, I found I was smiling too. And wouldn't you know it, by the time I left the restroom I too found my hand meeting hers for a high-five.

This is about as clear a purpose example as I can imagine. Though I'm fairly sure her purpose wasn't *to be a restroom attendant*, I'm quite certain that her purpose **was** *to bring joy,* or *to uplift*, or *to give*, or any number of purposes. The fact that she clearly knew her purpose, and found a way to incorporate it in her daily life, made all the difference for her and everyone she encountered.

What Exactly *Is* Purpose and Why Am I Hearing So Much About It?

There are many ways we can define purpose and/or meaning for our lives. I happen to like to use an adaptation of the textbook definition: the reason for which someone is created or exists.

Yes, I'm fully aware that determining the reason for your creation and existence can be more than a little daunting. Not to worry, though—figuring it out isn't something that will require that you quit your job, sell all your stuff, and travel to another land! Let's take this one step at a time and start with the **benefits** of determining your purpose. Then we'll dive into the actual process of pinpointing what your purpose may be, and how you can start to put it into practice to make your way toward Living in Bliss.

The Purpose of Purpose

Knowing your purpose is very much like holding a large map in your hand and circling a destination. Once you know **where** you'd like to go, you can then choose **how** you'd like to travel and the routes that are available. In other words, once you know **what** your purpose is, you can decide what types of activities, hobbies, career, volunteer work, and even friendships and relationships will be the right choices for helping you reach your destination.

Have you ever joined a committee or organization solely because *someone else* thought you'd be a good fit? I probably don't need to ask how that went, because I too have been down that road. When we engage in an activity or launch a career (or relationship) that isn't in alignment with our own purpose or interests, the effort is likely to end up in boredom, frustration, anxiety, and even resentment. At a minimum, it certainly isn't going to wind up as being the reason you get out of bed every day! And that means it's not taking you toward the bliss that you're here to find.

That's not to say that you might not unexpectedly find that you're genuinely engaged in something you didn't anticipate to be of interest. It *is* to say, though, that unless you're engaged, you should do yourself a favor and cut it out of your life.

Many years ago, I joined an organization and accepted a position on the executive board, solely because a dear friend of mine was on the board and thought it would be a good experience for us to do it together. I had no real interest in the organization (though they do great work), but agreed that it could be fun. Wouldn't you know, within the year my friend resigned from the board, while I begrudgingly continued to serve the rest of my term—resenting every moment. Looking back, I had no one to blame but myself. I knew that my interests weren't at the level they should have been in order to maintain the momentum to continue attending meetings and upholding my duties to the board. And yet, my mouth said "Yes" even when my heart said "No!!"

In the end, I had to admit that it was making me miserable, and that I'd done it for the wrong reasons. And then I had to opt out of an additional term, because being on that board wasn't the best use of my time or putting me on the path toward finding my purpose. It also wasn't helping the organization, because I'm sure they must have sensed my internal struggle through my lack of enthusiasm!

When you're clear on your purpose and passion (more on passion in the next chapter), you can spare yourself the frustration of wasted time and effort, and more clearly and freely focus on efforts in which you're willing to invest your whole heart! You'll find saying "No" much easier because you won't have to question your choices as you might otherwise have done. If you know your purpose, you'll know instinctively whether something will serve it or not. Additionally, your **work becomes more meaningful, your play becomes more relaxing and reenergizing, and relationships become more authentic and fulfilling when you're doing what you know you were meant to be doing.**

But how exactly do you figure that purpose out? Read on, and I'll give you some tips!

Discovering Your Purpose Doesn't Have to Be Painful

Yes, determining your purpose is a lofty goal, and a decision that ranks pretty high up there on the list of "Most Important Things to Do." While that's true, it's also true that your purpose doesn't need to be wildly monumental, as in "My purpose is to end starvation in the world." Or "My purpose is to rescue all of the unwanted pets in the world and pair them up with every child in need of a friend." Not to say these aren't phenomenal undertakings, only that they're incredibly aspirational and likely fall under the heading of dreams and visions (which can be created as a way of bringing your purpose to life).

Your purpose should be viewed as a more basic motivation that *acts as the driver* for your goals, dreams, and visions. Knowing this, the simplest answer is likely the best. For example, your purpose may be *to serve* or *to be the voice of humanity*, which may **drive** you to undertake fighting to end starvation, or to pair all of the unwanted pets with every child in need of a friend. Another example of purpose may be *to guide*, which may **drive** you to write a book, become a speaker, or lead retreats as a way of bringing your purpose to fruition.

Carin Rockind, a leading happiness and life purpose expert,[36] defines purpose as "Your unique way of impacting the world in a way that lights you up and therefore lights others up." Carin describes her unique perspective on purpose hunting as **"The Theory of Nouns."**

Somewhere along the line we started connecting purpose to job titles. Rather than saying "I want to be a fireman or a mom, or a

---

[36]Carin Rockind is the creator of PurposeGirl, a movement to empower purpose-driven living. Carin can be found on Stars Radio, Serious XM 109 morning show, *Wake up with Taylor*, and at www.purposegirl.com or at Twitter@Carinrockind.

teacher," **stop looking to fulfill your purpose with one noun. You're not just one thing**, *but rather a person with a purpose that is a verb; try looking at your purpose as a verb that starts with "to." For example: to lead, to inspire, to teach, to guide, etc.* **The how you're going to do this can be through multiple roles and opportunities.**

When you're focusing in on your purpose, there are hundreds upon hundreds of possibilities to choose from, a few of which I've included here.

—To nurture
—To serve
—To provide humor
—To enlighten
—To be the voice of reason
—To learn
—To care
—To listen
—To show humanity
—To activate potential
—To instill order
—To preserve life
—To provide clarity
—To instill justice
—To love
—To give hope
—To believe
…. **And the list goes on . . .**

Keep in mind that identifying your purpose is completely up to *you*. No one else can determine this for you, which means *no one can tell you that you've chosen incorrectly*.

I'd recommend looking at your life up to this point as a way to start identifying some of the patterns that may give clues as to what your purpose may be. For example, for as long as I can remember, my family told me that I always had to be in charge in our home. At work, I always felt I had to be the one to explain how to do certain tasks and help co-workers get more comfortable in a new role. In my personal life, I've always had an inclination to help friends find ways to solve problems they were facing or share information I found useful. Ultimately, I realized that my purpose was to guide. I suppose it could also be to lead or to inspire, but "to guide" is the one that resonates most with me. Another example: I have a client who once taught elementary school kids, then later worked as an independent product representative, and currently writes training manuals for a manufacturing company. What we ultimately discovered together is that his purpose is *to clarify*. Knowing that is what he likes to do, he can tailor his career (and/or hobbies, etc.) to include ways to help people more easily and successfully understand complicated information.

So as you're thinking about what your purpose may be (keeping in mind it may not be on the list of examples included here), start by looking for clues/patterns in your personal and professional life.

Exercise - Uncovering Clues

See examples 1 and 2, and then use the spaces in the column on the left to list a few of your past or current "roles" (in your personal and professional life) that may help you discover a pattern or clues as to what your purpose is. In the spaces on the right side, write down what you believe to be the clues and themes.

EXAMPLE 1:

MIDDLE CHILD

MEDIATOR

HOSTAGE NEGOTIATOR

EXAMPLE 2:

BABYSITTER

SCHOOL COUNSELOR

RED CROSS VOLUNTEER

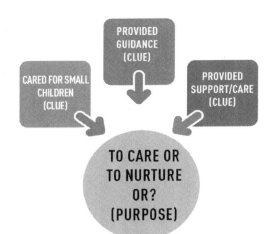

FILL IN YOUR ANSWERS HERE

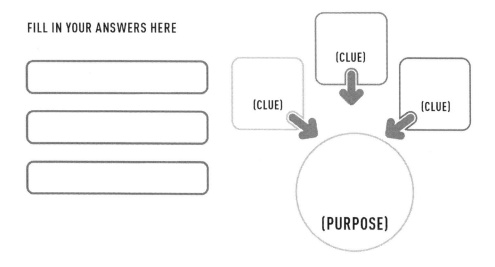

I won't pretend that uncovering your purpose won't require a little detective work and patience. But remember, there is no "perfect" choice to be had, and as a recovering perfectionist, I can tell you with certainty that when you drop the need for perfection you'll likely be happier and more satisfied with your choice. Try a purpose on for a few days and see how it fits. If it feels right, and makes you happy, then chances are you've uncovered yours. If it itches, though, or doesn't fit right, then try something else. And at the end of the day, realize that you might have more than one purpose, and that your purpose might change over time.

As long as you're moving toward satisfying what your purpose is at that moment in time, though, you'll be moving toward Living in Bliss, rather than working to impress others or creating a reputation that doesn't actually represent *who you really are*.

Don't Let Perfection Put Your Purpose on Pause

Since I've broached the P word (perfection), let's just go there for a moment. If you've ever suffered from having perfectionist tendencies, you've no doubt noticed that it seldom leads to bliss. My theory is that that's because perfectionists are often focused on what could've or might've been, rather than what actually *is* (i.e., this day at the beach would be perfect **if** it were 5 degrees cooler. This dinner out would've been perfect **if** I could've sat at *that* table instead of this one. The work I'm doing would be really meaningful **if** I could get more people to agree with my ideas).

Now, before I lead you down the path of condemning your inner perfectionist, let me be the first to say that there are definitely times when listening to that part of your inner wisdom is **exactly** what you may want to do. While I'm often aware of (and purposely resisting) my constant inclination to make something just a little bit better, it has definitely been a huge asset when it comes to my career path, desire to learn new things, and drive to guide myself and others from good to great. The important thing is to know whether you're inclined to have perfectionist tendencies, and when and how to turn that urge off when it isn't useful. Because when it comes to uncovering your purpose, it's important to ensure that you don't get so caught up in analysis that you end up in paralysis.

So let's do a little pre-work before further exploring and pinpointing your purpose, just to see if you may or may not be inclined to reach for perfection when it comes to decision making.

Exercise - Prone to Perfection?

Not sure whether you're prone to perfection? Take a look at this simple self-quiz,[37] on the next page, to determine where you fall on the "Maximizer Scale." Remember, to get the most out of the exercise, you'll need to be completely honest with your answers.

---

[37] Schwartz, B. "Maximizing Versus Satisficing: Happiness Is a Matter of..." 2002 http://www.wisebrain.org/media/Papers/maximizing.pdf

EXERCISE – MAXIMIZER / *SATISFICER SCALE

1	2	3	4	5	6	7

COMPLETELY DISAGREE   AGREE   COMPLETELY AGREE

LIST YOUR ANSWER, USING THE SCALE ABOVE.

	No matter how satisfied I am with my job, it's only right for me to be on the lookout for better opportunities.
	When I'm in the car listening to the radio, I often check other stations to see if something better is playing, even if I'm relatively satisfied with what I'm listening to.
	When I watch TV I channel surf, often scanning through the available option even while attempting to watch one program.
	I treat relationships like clothing; I expect to try a lot on before finding the perfect fit.
	I often find it difficult to shop for a gift for a friend.
	Renting videos is really difficult. I'm always struggling to pick the best one.
	When shopping, I have a hard time finding clothing that I really love .
	I'm a big fan of lists that attempt to rank things (the best movies, the best songs, the best athletes, the best books, etc.).
	I find that writing is very difficult, even if it's just writing a letter to a friend, because it's so hard to word things just right. I often do several drafts of even the simplest things.
	I never settle for second best.
	Whenever I'm faced with a choice, I try to imagine what all the other possibilities are, even ones that aren't present at the moment.
	I often fantasize about living in ways that are quite different from my actual life.
	No matter what I do, I have the highest standards for myself.
	RECORD THE SUM OF YOUR ANSWERS IN THE BOX TO THE LEFT.

*Yes, the spelling for Satisficer is correct, I promise.

Add the sum of your answers and place your total in the box to the left of the "total" box. Use the guide below to see where you fall on the scale.

And the Answer Is . . .

—Totals points range from 13-91
—65 or higher are Maximizers
—40 or lower are Satisficers
—People who have taken the test range from 25-75, with an average of 50 points, and no difference between women and men

Note that a Maximizer is defined as "Someone who is more prone toward social comparison, less confident in their decisions, more likely to experience regret due to forgone opportunities or hypothetical options, and more interested in making the perfect choice . . . to the point of weighing every possible option at great length."

In other words, a Maximizer may have a difficult time not only making decisions, but also being satisfied with the choice once they've made it.

Satisficers[38] may also be mistaken for Maximizers simply because they typically know the criteria and what they're looking for, and likely won't settle until they've found something very close to what they're looking for. Satisficers are not described as people who are "settling," but rather as people who are satisfied with the choices they've made. "They're generally happier with their decisions, experience less regret and stress, and spend more time on things that they feel are more important to them."

---

[38] Yes, I know the spelling looks odd, but it's correct, I promise.

I've suggested that you determine whether you may lean more toward Maximizer or Satisficer because, after helping clients determine their purpose for more than a decade, more often than not I've seen a well-intending, successful person freeze in their tracks when faced with the selection of what their purpose may be because they are so concerned with making sure that they've made the absolutely correct/perfect choice. They may be tempted not to make any choice at all for fear of being "wrong." The downside to that "solution" is that it's nearly impossible to hit the target if you don't know where it is. In other words, how can you know which roles, responsibilities, and opportunities to choose if you're unclear on what will satisfy your soul?

But when your soul is satisfied, you're on your way to creating a purposeful, engaged, and pleasurable existence. Which means it's important to figure that out.

Tips for Painless Purpose Exploration

It's no wonder so many freeze, when there's so much to consider! The problem is, too many choices can create decision fatigue and anxiety, and as I just mentioned, many decide not to choose at all, for fear of making a "bad choice." What's important is to stop "getting ready to get ready," and avoid the temptation to put your life on "hold" while you're waiting for the perfect purpose to reveal itself. If you want to move forward with a blissful life and finding your well being, you have to get over your perfectionism and make a move!

Carin Rockind's Tips for Exploring Your Purpose

—Dispense with the nouns. Stop asking yourself if you should *be* a teacher, doctor, architect, etc., for at least a few weeks. Don't base your purpose on a career, because you'll base your definition of the role on what you've predetermined it to be, and will limit yourself greatly. Instead, think of your purpose as a verb that typically starts with "to" (to guide, teach, inspire, etc.)

—**Shift your language.** When you've spent time unsuccessfully searching for your purpose (after the age of twenty-three), it's depressing! In fact, it can even create "purpose anxiety," because searching equates with loss, and may shift you into fight or flight mode. This mode cuts off your creativity, higher-level thinking, and digestive system, and in that space/stress mode, we can't find our purpose or access anything larger than ourselves. Change your language so that it eliminates the words "search" or "find." They're stressful words. Use instead words like "explore" and "uncover," which are more about curiosity. Curiosity is a positive emotion, and research shows us that positive emotions allow us to open our minds to broader horizons.

—**Get in touch with what inspires and lifts you up**. Think about the last time you were inspired or felt uplifted. This helps you get in touch with what it feels like when you're more alive. This will also help you differentiate between what juices you up and what sucks you dry. When you're contributing and you're lit up, you're on purpose. Your body, and the way you feel, always tells you the answer. That is what your purpose is. That's the direction in which you need to travel. On the other hand, if you feel drained and uninspired, it's likely you're headed in the wrong direction and in need of a course correction.

—**Notice the themes**. Take notice of what you're doing, who you're doing it with, and the ways that you're naturally showing up in the world, personally and professionally. Think about what you wanted to do or be when you were a kid. Who, what, why did you want to serve? Notice any themes?

—Focus on what you can give, rather than what you can take.

—Start where you are. If you're in a professional role and you're frustrated because you're not doing something that feels meaningful, find ways of bringing the meaningful things into your role. If your calling is to guide or uplift or inspire, for example, look to see if you're already doing that. If you're not, it might be why you're frustrated. Live your purpose with everyone—that's where it starts.

You may also find these additional tips helpful:

Tip 1: Pick a few options and try them on for size
See which purpose resonates with you and how you feel about it. As you begin to bring more of your true purpose into your life, you may notice your sense of fulfillment and happiness increasing as a result. You have nothing to lose in the trial stage, and everything to gain!

Tip 2: Don't include specific people or places in your purpose statement (i.e., My purpose is to take care of my kids). When we make our purpose dependent upon someone or something else, what happens when that person/thing is no longer in need of your services (kids are grown, business, charity, or organization has reorganized or closed their doors, divorce has occurred)? This is where those who are faced with an empty nest, retirement, or "down sizing" at work can find themselves feeling completely lost and without purpose. Rather than saying, "My purpose is to take care of my kids," you might try saying, "My purpose is to serve," or "My purpose is to nurture." Instead of saying "My purpose is to be the best

CEO this company has ever had," try saying, "My purpose is to lead with inspiration."

Tip 3: When you're determining your purpose, you may find it useful to practice "unconscious decision-making." Unconscious decision-making occurs when you've gathered important data about yourself and the decision to be made, and the options, and then purposely go about doing something else to distract yourself while your mind unconsciously reviews the options. In other words, don't agonize about the decision. Studies show that unconscious decisions are typically more effective than conscious decisions when there are more than four options from which to choose.[39]

Tip 4: Never let anyone else tell you who you are. This tip is one that sits close to my heart. For years I let other people tell me who I was (or at least, who *they* thought I was). The problem was, their definition wasn't always a noble or accurate one. But for a long time, I believed them. They'd tell me that I was picky or bossy, or sarcastic, or whatever. Somewhere in my thirties, I decided that I really didn't like the persona that had been created and it was time to change that story. I realized that many of us have the potential to demonstrate sarcastic or bossy behaviors, but that doesn't have to dictate *who* we are. So I did some digging, defined who *I knew myself to be,* and decided to believe *that.* When I realized that my purpose was to guide (with joy), it became a filter for my actions. Sarcasm and bossiness might be a small piece of what makes me whole, but we *are not our first thought.* I know that both instincts can be harmful, and aren't

---

[39]Dijksterhuis, Ap. "Think different: the merits of unconscious thought in preference development and decision making." *Journal of personality and social psychology* 87.5 (2004): 586

in alignment with my true self, and I purposely *choose* behaviors, words, and actions that accurately demonstrate who I really am and how I want to show up in this world. No matter what your age, or how long you've known the people around you (at work or home), you can decide to change your story and do it. Now. When you're living in alignment with your purpose, and you're careful to ensure that your actions and words accurately reflect that purpose, you'll find that your life *will begin to feel more like the experience you want it to be.* Which, by the way, feels pretty darn blissful.

Tip 5: Silence please. But there's more to it than just not listening to the people who try to dictate who you are. One of the best ways to go about listening for clues to your purpose is to stop listening to everything else going on around you. Turn off the TV, radio, Internet, telephone, text, and even your own chatter, and just listen. It might be different, uncomfortable, or even a little scary to embrace the quiet, but the benefit can be substantial. As Max Ehrmann puts it so elegantly, "Go placidly among the noise and haste and remember what peace there may be in silence." When you get quiet, you start to allow room to hear what your inner wisdom may be trying to tell you. We'll cover more on the process of capturing your inner wisdom shortly.

Tip 6: Be authentic.

"Authenticity means letting go of who we think we're supposed to be and embracing who we actually are." —Brene' Brown[40]

---

[40] "Brené Brown Quotes (Author of The Gifts of Imperfection)," 2011, http://www.goodreads.com/author/quotes/162578.Bren_Brown (accessed April 15, 2016).

I'm quite certain that my purpose is to guide with hope and joy. However, for years and years I pushed aside the work of helping others identify and live their bliss because my ego wouldn't hear of it. In 2007, the economy crashed just when I left my twenty-year career with a Fortune 50 company to start my own business. You can bet there was *no way* I was going to lose my self respect by offering what I feared others would scoff at when times were tight everywhere. So I pushed aside the vision I had for my purpose, and pursued straight consulting, training, and executive coaching. And while my checkbook and ego were fulfilled, my heart was not. The longer I ignored the vision for my purpose, the emptier I felt. It wasn't until I addressed my ego *and* soul, and incorporated the work of purpose, engagement, happiness, and self-care into my corporate offerings, that I felt a sense of fulfillment begin to reside where my inner struggle had existed for years.

Tip 7: Stop letting your ego boss you around.

"Life can be pulled by goals just as surely as it can be pushed by drives." —Viktor Frankl, author of Man's Search for Meaning[41]

I've mentioned the inner struggle between my ego and soul—my soul wanted me to find meaning and purpose in my career, and my ego was most interested in looking credible and being successful according to other people's standards. Not surprisingly, this is the point where many people find themselves conflicted. For example, your soul may tell you that your purpose is to demonstrate care, in which case you may begin to think about how you can act on that purpose. Maybe you could volunteer to serve meals at a homeless

---

[41] "Life can be pulled by goals just as surely as it can be ... – BrainyQuote," http://www.brainyquote.com/quotes/quotes/v/viktorefr153413.html

shelter or donate items to a local charity. Great—you're on to something and you feel pretty good! However, it is at this point that your ego may jump in with both feet to up the ante. Why should you stop at volunteering to serve meals locally? That's hardly noteworthy (according to your ego). Why not sign on to join a mission trip to another country, or better yet, *lead* a group on a mission trip?! That would r*eally look great,* wouldn't it?

At which point you may find that you become completely overwhelmed and decide that you don't really have time or energy for any of it, and put it off until things settle down.

As I've stated before, the ego can be incredibly helpful when it comes to inspiring action (and getting you off the couch or out of bed). Your ego pushes you to do great work and take care of yourself. However, when it becomes so invasive that it actually rules how you live, or keeps you from doing things that nurture your soul, you're on a slippery slope that will likely wind up in a state of anxiety and turmoil (if it hasn't already).

Exercise - Bringing Your Purpose Into Focus

Now that you have a little background on how to begin determining your purpose, let's start to visualize what your purpose may be.

What you'll need:
—Pen and paper
—Quiet space
—Three to five minutes (or longer) of quiet time
—Recording device (optional)

First, pull out your paper and pen and get your timer set for three minutes. Next, you may want to record the directions listed here, so that you can play them back as you complete the exercise with your eyes closed.

Now, place your feet on the floor, sit or stand in a comfortable position, and close your eyes. During the next three minutes, I'd like you to begin to imagine yourself on your *very best day*. You can be anywhere in the world you'd like to be, doing anything you choose. You could be working, playing, volunteering—whatever you decide. On this day you're looking and feeling fantastic! Really let yourself absorb the feeling. Now, start to make out the details of what you're doing . . . are you with other people or alone? Indoors or out? What are you doing? How do others see you, and how do you see yourself? Are you providing a service? Are you writing, speaking, painting, serving, or maybe creating? Can you make out any of the details? Again, notice how you're *feeling*. Can you make out what you're contributing? Try to focus as best you can, and don't worry if it seems fuzzy or if your mind jumps around to different scenarios. All the information is useful.

Next, open your eyes, and for the next one to two minutes, write down everything you can remember. I find it helpful to use bullet points, for example:

—I'm outside, in a beautiful garden area.
—There are many people around, men and women.
—I feel connected and energized, fit and graceful.
—I see myself talking with the group, guiding and sharing stories.
—People are enjoying the experience and chiming in with their stories.
—We laugh sometimes and think deeply. They feel motivated and inspired.

—I see myself talking on the phone and through video and community, somehow guiding and providing support.
—My heart is full and I am energized!

Keep in mind, my list was compiled after doing this exercise a few times. You may have an extensive list or only one or two bullets (or parts of a bullet), and the thoughts may seem entirely disconnected. Collect details and write them all down, without judgment or anxiety, until you feel you have a reasonable amount of information to work with.

Remember: Try to resist the temptation to imagine what others may expect or want from you. This is a purely self-centered exercise (you are **centering** yourself) and you don't need to feel the least bit guilty about what you envision. Right now you're just collecting information.

Don't worry if you haven't discovered your purpose at this point—there's no need for extra stress! Jot down any notes or feelings that may be a clue as to what your purpose might be.

My Purpose Is to:

_____

_____

Notes: _____

_____

_____

_____

CHAPTER FIVE

Go With the Flow

"Twenty years from now you will be more disappointed by the things that you didn't do than by the ones you did do. So throw off the bowlines. Sail away from the safe harbor. Catch the trade winds in your sails. Explore. Dream. Discover." –Mark Twain

As we move through the process of creating a life that's a balance of purpose, engagement, and pleasure, the next logical step is to move into passion and ultimately flow, which are closely linked to all three components.

Without purpose and passion, our lives would no doubt be one continuous, monotonous race to the finish line. I can, without hesitation, say that recognizing the need for purpose and passion in your life is what sets you apart from the rest of the population. Sometimes this may be a blessing, and sometimes it may be a curse, depending on how you look at it. There have definitely been times in my life when I would have been *more than happy* to feel completely content with the status quo. Ah, but that is not the path that my heart is content to take and, in all honesty, I wouldn't have it any other way.

When I talk about passion, I'm not talking about the X-rated kind (though that would make for an interesting topic), but rather the kind of passion that drives us *out of bed* in the morning. Passion can be closely related to our purpose, and when the two are combined we have the potential to hit "flow" stage, which we'll talk more about in this chapter.

Passion is often a misunderstood emotion. For our use, though, we'll define it as **anything that peaks your interest, commands your attention, and dominates your desire to invest more time and energy.** Additionally, I want to clarify that when I refer to passion, I'm talking about the *harmonious* variety of passion (the type that contributes to a positive life) rather than the *obsessive* variety of passion (the type that, when taken to the extreme, creates a negative impact on your life). Let's take a closer look at what passion might be, and how you can identify your own, so that you can take the next steps toward finding your bliss. After all, if you don't know what you're passionate about, how are you going to know what makes you happy?

Putting Your Finger on the Pulse of Your Passion

Oftentimes when I'm working with a client, I notice that as we approach the topic of passion they may become shy, reserved, and maybe even intimidated by the exercise, possibly because they feel it's too selfish to focus on something that is about them and only them. However, as I mentioned above, passion goes a long way toward creating a life of bliss because it's one of the few components that relates solely to what you *most enjoy doing*. So no, it isn't selfish, it's self "centered"—in the best way possible—because the whole reason for engaging in the activity is to bring joy, fun, challenge, energy, peace, and anything else that makes you feel alive and centered into your life! Think of your experiences like this: every experience is either a deposit into or a withdrawal from your "bank of resilience." When you add more of what you're passionate about into your daily life, you're making deposits and you're better able to build your capacity and resilience. By doing so, you're more easily able to mentally spring into action when you're dealing with the activities and responsibilities that you *don't* necessarily feel passionate about. It's this Yin and Yang of passion and responsibility that make up the whole idea of creating "balance" in your life. And where there is balance, there is opportunity for bliss.

Exercise - Passion Pulse

Use this opportunity to identify your known and yet-to-be discovered opportunities for passion. Keep in mind that this exercise is *all about you*, and is not the place to hold back on what really has the potential for bringing more of what you love into your daily life. I've included sample categories to help inspire your exploration. Again, don't hold back on this exercise, and avoid the temptation to try to figure out how or *if* it's even possible to accomplish your wish list. We'll get to that later!

EXAMPLES - PASSION PULSE

THINGS YOU LOVE TO DO	THINGS YOU WANT TO TRY	THINGS YOU THINK YOU WANT TO TRY	PLACES YOU WANT TO GO	EXPERIENCES YOU WANT TO HAVE	ANYTHING ELSE?
Spa!	Take a cooking class	Sushi?	Italy!	Live in Italy for a month!	Take an online shorthand class to brush up on my skills
Dining out	Learn to play piano	Water skiing?	Vancouver BC to visit a friend	Speak at destination spas and resorts	Get to know my son's friends better
Professional speaking!	Learn to speak Italian	Write a book	The new park downtown	Lead getaway retreats in beautiful places!	

FILL IN YOUR ANSWERS BELOW:

THINGS YOU LOVE TO DO	THINGS YOU WANT TO TRY	THINGS YOU THINK YOU WANT TO TRY	PLACES YOU WANT TO GO	EXPERIENCES YOU WANT TO HAVE	ANYTHING ELSE?

Were you able to capture a few things you know you'd like to do or try? How about a few things you *think* you might like to try? If so, use this space to set your intention to do at least three of the things you'd most like to do within the next thirty days.

EXAMPLE:

I will do/try **taking a cooking class** (activity) by **April 30** (date) with **Amy** (anyone joining you?) because I know that doing so will bring more **spice** (joy/happiness/fun/peace, etc.) into my life!

FILL IN YOUR INTENTIONS BELOW:

I will do/try _____ (activity) by_____ (date) with _____ (anyone joining you?) because I know that doing so will bring more _____ (joy/happiness/fun/peace, etc.) into my life!

I will do/try _____ (activity) by_____ (date) with _____ (anyone joining you?) because I know that doing so will bring more _____ (joy/happiness/fun/peace, etc.) into my life!

I will do/try _____ (activity) by_____ (date) with _____ (anyone joining you?) because I know that doing so will bring more _____ (joy/happiness/fun/peace, etc.) into my life!

Great, you're on a roll! Ready to try a little stretch exercise to further your growth? I'm thinking you might be up for the challenge. If so, continue on . . .

EXERCISE - PASSION STRETCH!

THINGS YOU THINK YOU WANT TO TRY	WITH WHO?	BY WHAT DATE?	PREDICT YOUR EXPERIENCE SATISFACTION (0-100%)	HOW MUCH DID YOU ACTUALLY ENJOY THE EXPERIENCE?
Try Sushi for the first time?	My husband	March 30, 2016	I'm 10% likely to enjoy eating Sushi	Wow! I actually kind of liked it! 70% enjoyed Sushi.
Write a book	Just me	October 2015	20% likely to enjoy the process	This was an awesome experience! 95% enjoyed the experience!

USE THE TABLE BELOW TO FILL IN YOUR OWN STRETCH AND GROW EXPERIENCE

THINGS YOU THINK YOU WANT TO TRY	WITH WHO?	BY WHAT DATE?	PREDICT YOUR EXPERIENCE SATISFACTION (0-100%)	HOW MUCH DID YOU ACTUALLY ENJOY THE EXPERIENCE?

Hopefully, you now have a clearer picture of what experiences bring or *might* bring more passion into your life. If not, that's ok too—we certainly don't want to give you more things to stress about! You can always come back later to fill in additional pieces of information. You may want to reach out to your family to ask them to remind you of the things that you enjoyed or got excited about as a kid or young adult. You can also ask your close friends to remind you of what they've noticed catching your interest or lighting you up. Keep in mind, identifying and incorporating what you might be passionate about into your life will now be part of your ongoing routine. Bliss often comes on the heels of passion, and can definitely bring more happiness into your life!

In the Zone

Have you ever been so engaged in what you're doing that you literally lose all track of time? You may've been dancing, surfing, painting, reading, writing, jogging, giving a presentation, playing with your kids, engaged in a conversation, doing volunteer work, or anything else that draws you back again and again (yes, sex too). According to Hungarian psychologist, Mihaly Csikszentmihalyi,[42] when you're engaged in passion that demands a highly focused mental state, you may reach a state of "flow," also known as being "in the zone."

My husband, Larry, is incredibly passionate about tennis. I've seen him play two tournaments back to back (a total of four hours of play), with a badly twisted ankle and no rest or food, in 90+ degree temperatures. What sounds like

---

[42] "Mihaly Csikszentmihalyi - Pursuit of Happiness," 2010, http://www.pursuit-of-happiness.org/history-of-happiness/mihaly-csikszentmihalyi/ (accessed February 16, 2016).

pure agony to me is his definition of pure bliss. When it's minus 12 degrees and snowing outside, he'll find an indoor court. When we're on vacation, he'll book a tennis lesson to ensure he has time on the court wherever we go. Additionally, he says playing tennis and "being in the zone" helps him clear his mind of everything else and gain perspective to make better decisions *off* the court. This goes back to the example I gave you in the last chapter about making decisions with the subconscious mind.

Beyond clearing your mind, frequent "flow" is associated with more life satisfaction, a sense of achievement, better health, and greater creativity. Through flow, we can also experience a decrease in pain symptoms and "a natural, productive high." And when you're able to create all these positive feelings, while doing something you love to do, you're engaged in, and in which you're finding pleasure—all at the same time—this is where you'll likely experience bliss.

But to do that, you have to have some idea of what you're passionate *about* so that you can use that information to create your own flow.

I can't remember a time when my son wasn't wildly passionate about playing the drums. He has literally loved playing since he was old enough to beat out a tune on *anything, anywhere.* He's a young adult now, and recently had the opportunity to sit in with a very successful local cover band, who afterward asked if he might be interested in being a permanent substitute for their drummer. *Might* be interested? When he called to tell me his news, I could practically *feel* his excitement buzzing through the phone! He told me that he knew it was going to be a challenge and that he'd have to work to make sure they felt they could really trust him as a backup—and he was more than ready to prove it to them! Yes, he was definitely hitting his flow and I couldn't be happier for him; his excitement was infectious! I realized that in both his and Larry's examples, their experience of flow came from doing something they were truly passionate about while mastering a new challenge. They know what they're passionate about, and they go after it in their pursuit of bliss.

One of the great things about flow is that it's pretty easy to recognize: You may feel joyous and/or energized, or completely immersed in the process, despite the fact that the activity may be physically or mentally demanding. But that's how you'll know that you're truly in a state of flow—no matter how much work or energy it takes, you're up for the challenge. It's worth pointing out that you can experience passion without hitting a state of flow (ie, you're enjoying a really great meal or listening to music you really enjoy). And you can experience flow without necessarily feeling passion (ie, riding a bicycle around a congested area of town, being highly skilled at a challenging task at work, or exercising to a difficult routine you know well). The important aspect is to get to that state where your skill level meets the challenge and it happens so naturally that there's no interference from your thinking mind.

Some of the key components of "flow" are as follows[43]:

—There are clear goals every step of the way

—There is immediate feedback to one's actions

—There is a balance between challenges and skills

—Action and awareness are merged

—Distractions are excluded from consciousness

—There's no worry of failure

—Self-consciousness disappears

—The sense of time becomes distorted (you lose all track of time)

---

[43] "Csikszentmihalyi and Happiness - Pursuit of Happiness." 2010 http://www.pursuit-of-happiness.org/history-of-happiness/mihaly-csikszentmihalyi/ (accessed April 28, 2016).

It might seem counterintuitive, but many people enjoy their work more than their free time because there are built in goals, rules, feedback, and challenges. This is typically when you'll hear people say, "Work doesn't feel like work at all!" And it's because there's structure in place that makes it flow, and keeps people in the moment and engaged. That flow can make even the most difficult tasks rewarding.

Alternatively, unstructured free time can actually make us feel bored, restless, anxious, and possibly even as if we're in physical pain. This is why it can be critical for many people to have at least a little structure and/or pre-planning, passion, and flow activities built into vacations, extended time off, or retirement—so that there are opportunities to feel challenged, engaged, and invigorated. Optimally, you want to strive for adding *both kinds of experiences* (passion and flow) into your personal and professional life. Without those positive feelings, it can be far more difficult to create a happy, if not blissful, life. And when you're navigating a new opportunity or phase in your life, you want to ensure that you've set yourself up as well as possible for positive experiences that translate into a positive existence.

Take a look at Csikszentmihalyi's "Flow" chart,[44] which helps to illustrate why we might feel the way we do when we're working or playing. You'll also see how it's possible to move from boredom to high interest, and even flow state, simply by increasing the challenge level (provided you have the coordinating skill).

---

[44] "Mihaly Csikszentmihalyi—Wikipedia, the free encyclopedia," 2011, https://en.wikipedia.org/wiki/Mihaly_Csikszentmihalyi (accessed February 16, 2016).

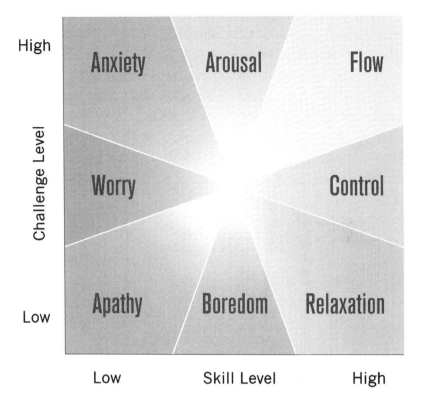

A client of mine confided in me that she was in a business partnership where she often felt anxious, frustrated, and unable to successfully influence any given situation. In fact, she felt so anxious that her confidence in her professional skills had dropped to an all-time low, despite the fact that her income had reached an all-time high. When I asked her to step back and take a look at the flow chart, she realized that the skills and talent she brought to the partnership were not being utilized—and so she felt a strong sense of apathy for the projects she took part in. Additionally, the projects commanded a high-challenge level of skills that she had not honed (and had no interest in honing), leaving her with the understandable feeling of anxiety and frustration. To alleviate the anxiety and increase her interest, she would either need to increase her skill level to match the challenge or adjust her involvement in the project to fit her skills and interests. Ultimately, she opted to pursue alternate projects where she was able to throw her passion and skills into full use. Not coincidentally, she tells me she has never been happier.

EXERCISE - GO WITH THE FLOW

Use Csikszentmihalyi's "Flow Chart" to examine an area of your personal or professional life where you experience flow.

WRITE YOUR "FLOW" EXAMPLE HERE. (Example: I reach flow state when I water ski and try new tricks):

NEXT, WRITE DOWN WHY YOU BELIEVE YOU REACH FLOW WHEN DOING THIS ACTIVITY.

(Example: I constantly increase my skill level to meet or exceed the challenge level. When I've reached a goal, I increase the challenge):

NOW, THINK OF AN AREA OF YOUR LIFE THAT YOU'D LIKE TO IMPROVE. (Examples: I'm feeling bored with a current aspect of my career. I'm feeling anxious about delivering a presentation or project for a client):

NEXT, IDENTIFY WHERE EITHER THE CHALLENGE LEVEL OR YOUR SKILL LEVEL MAY BE TOO LOW OR TWO HIGH. OF AN AREA OF YOUR LIFE THAT YOU'D LIKE TO IMPROVE. (Example: If you're feeling bored with a current aspect of your career, it could be that the challenge level is lower than your skill level. If you're feeling anxious about delivering a presentation or project, it could be that you don't yet possess the level of skill needed to meet the demand—so you may want to build your skills):

LASTLY, IDENTIFY WHERE YOU CAN MAKE ADJUSTMENTS TO IMPROVE HOW YOU FEEL ABOUT YOUR EXAMPLE. (For instance: To decrease anxiety about delivering a project, focus on either increasing your skill level or bringing in someone with expertise in that area to assist you with the delivery so that you're well equipped to match the requirements. If you're feeling bored, you may want to change things up to make the normal routines more interesting by doing things that challenge your skill level. What adjustments will you make?

Avoiding the Hedonic Hamster Wheel

So what's next in your steps toward Living in Bliss? Well, I really can't talk about passion without bringing up the importance of mindfulness and self-regulation. We live in an era where the opportunity and means to acquire more and more stuff is on an upward spiral; in fact, U.S. GNP per capita has risen by a factor of three since 1960. However, according to the World Happiness Report,[45] "the measures of average happiness have remained essentially unchanged over the half-century."

You may be asking yourself how that's possible, and you wouldn't be alone in that question. One of the reasons is that we may be suffering from decision fatigue. Simply put, we're exhausted from making too many decisions about too many things every day. From the variety of restaurants and types of food we want to eat, to social media and entertainment choices, the number of decisions you and I make in this decade is far greater than in any time period to date.

Yet even though the accumulation of experiences and things doesn't necessarily make us happier, we continue to acquire stuff, experiences, and social media profiles—which in turn necessitates that we bring in additional income, allocate more time, and accumulate more stress. We have to work harder to get those things that we claim to want, and the things don't make us any happier in the end, because we're having to work so hard to get them. It's a vicious cycle, and not one that leads us toward bliss.

I'm not suggesting that there's anything *wrong* with enjoying new experiences or things; heaven knows I love a

---

[45] World Happiness Report: Home," edited by John Helliwell, Richard Layard and Jeffrey Sachs, 2015, http://worldhappiness.report/ (accessed April 14, 2016).

great vacation, restaurant, clothes, etc., and I've encouraged you to get clear on what you're passionate about. What I *am* suggesting is that you may have accumulated more than you need in order to be happy. What if you, as a joy-seeking, fun-loving, successful person, took a step back and reassessed what is **truly** important in your life, and what truly makes you happy? Is it all those things? Probably not. Is it something deeper, which you've missed out on because you're preoccupied with getting new stuff? It's possible that might be the case—as it was for me and many of the clients I've coached.

Let me ask you this: Following the holidays or a vacation, have you ever found that you've enjoyed so much decadent food that you just can't indulge anymore? At that point, you may even decide to take part in a strict weight loss program. I have. It never ceases to amaze me how once I really focus on what I'd like the outcome to be (feeling more fit, healthy, and comfortable in my clothes), I'm able to more easily self-regulate my food intake. Whereas I may have previously consumed food with wild abandon, constantly trolling for the next tasty treat while on vacation (yes, it's been known to happen), over the course of a few disciplined days, I'm suddenly paying more attention to everything I eat and savoring every bite. I'll also willingly choose foods that help me feel full longer and more easily satisfy my cravings. At this point, it's no longer about quantity and variety of foods, it's now about *quality and enjoyment of what I consume*!

You can apply this same principal to the accumulation of *stuff* that you believe will make you happy. When I'm talking about passion and joy, it's about bringing in more quality of *life*, rather than quantity of *stuff* that may or may not make you happy in either the long or short term. In the example above, I choose to eat smaller portions of healthier food, to accomplish my goal. In terms of life, I choose to acquire only what will improve the quality of life, rather than every new gadget or indulgence that becomes available. See the connection there?

So what does all of this have to do with passion or purpose or flow, you're asking yourself? When you're more mindful of the activities and material goods you're bringing into your life (extravagant vacations, meals, clothes, fast food, cars, toys, etc.), and regulate how often you indulge in them, you create the conditions for less distraction and greater appreciation of the people, activities, experiences, and material goods that really matter to you and really do increase your quality of life. Additionally, once you've eliminated any excess that isn't making you truly happy, you can start to increase your available time, resources, and energy to add in opportunities and try out other interests that speak to your purpose and passion.

Consider this: What are one or two activities or material goods that you could easily eliminate in order to free up time, energy, and resources for more purposeful and passionate interests and investments?

_____

_____

Integrity and Character

When you completed the "Bringing Your Purpose Into Focus" exercise in the last chapter, there's a good chance you might have envisioned which *character strengths* you were displaying (knowledge, gratitude, hope, humor, love, honesty, etc.), rather than envisioning your actual purpose. And that's not unique to you. Christopher Peterson and Martin

Seligman,[46] leading researchers in the science of positive psychology, have identified 24 **Character Strengths** through compiling and reviewing thousands of pieces of scientific data from around the world. A true "Character Strength" is something that is morally valued and benefits others when it's displayed.

Additionally, to qualify as a Character Strength, it must consistently show up in your behaviors, thoughts, feelings, and actions, and ultimately contribute to a positive life for you and others. So you're not only adding to your own quality of life, you're adding to the quality of life of the people who engage with you. Now we're talking!

---

[46] Peterson, Christopher, and Martin EP Seligman. *Character strengths and virtues: A handbook and classification*. New York: Oxford University Press, 2004.

HERE ARE THE TWENTY-FOUR CHARACTER STRENGTHS

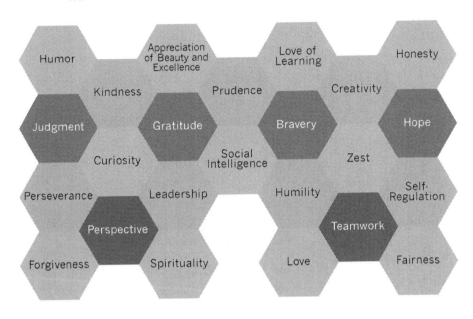

You'll notice that although some of the character strengths could be viewed as being a purpose (ie, love), they are truly actions, thoughts, and feelings that you may **demonstrate**. However, when you have an understanding of your character strengths, *and* an understanding of your purpose (the basic motivation that acts as a driver for your actions, thoughts, and feelings), you're on the right track to determining the kinds of work and play you are likely to find most meaningful to you. When you pair those up with passion and flow, you're on your way to bliss!!

To take the assessment to determine your top five Character Strengths, go to www.ViaCharacter.org. Remember, if you're being authentic (embracing who you really are) and living in integrity (in the right relationship with yourself), you'll *feel* when you're heading down the right path. When you're doing things you love, in a way that you feels good to you, you may discover your purpose *through* your passion (remember the singing restroom attendant from the last chapter?), which is an extra bonus because you know that doing what you love is also something you may have been born to do!

Keep in mind, it's important to pay attention to what you are genuinely attracted to, rather than what you *think you're supposed to be attracted to* (soul vs. ego) and follow your intuition. Again, this is a private decision and you're the **only one** who can decide if it feels right. If you feel a strong sense of unease (a mild/moderate sense is to be expected when you're making changes), then check in with your inner wisdom to ensure that you're listening to your true calling rather than a purely ego-driven endeavor. When you've reached an inner negotiation with your ego and soul, you'll likely feel a sense of relief or maybe an "aha!" moment. It doesn't mean that all will be perfect or that you may immediately know how to bring your purpose to life, but it is an excellent target for which to aim!

Let's use the next exercise to pull it all together.

EXERCISE - PULLING IT ALL TOGETHER

Use the following chart to identify how you can put your purpose, character strengths and passion into practice to bring you more purpose, engagement, and pleasure (bliss).

WHAT OUTCOME DO YOU WANT?	CHARACTER STRENGTHS (go to VIAcharacter.org)	PURPOSE (to guide, inspire, teach, love, etc.)	PASSION (sports, dining, outdoors, playing w/kids, etc.)	SECRET INTERESTS (an interest you've always wanted to explore)	NEXT STEPS?
ex.to feel relaxed	ex.appreciation for beauty	ex.to guide	ex.spending time in nature	ex.to take part in a retreat where they focus on relaxation and nature	ex.check into retreats that fit the criteria
ex.to feel energized	ex.humor and creativity	ex.to teach	ex.having fun with friends	ex.to put together a stand-up comedy routine	ex.do a search to find out how to get started
ex.to make a contribution	ex.kindness	ex.to show compassion	ex.being really involved in a project & seeing it through	ex.becoming a "big sister/big brother" volunteer	ex.check into local organizations and match with your availability

FILL IN YOUR ANSWERS BELOW:

WHAT OUTCOME DO YOU WANT?	CHARACTER STRENGTHS (go to VIAcharacter.org)	PURPOSE (to guide, inspire, teach, love, etc.)	PASSION (sports, dining, outdoors, playing w/kids, etc.)	SECRET INTERESTS (an interest you've always wanted to explore)	NEXT STEPS?

Once you've focused on what you *want more of*, you'll find it easier to eliminate whatever excess may be in your life. When you've accomplished both, you're well on your way to finding more purpose, engagement, and pleasure in your life! In other words, you're on your way to bliss!

Could You Use a Little Extra Guidance and Inspiration?

Feel free to reach out to me through my website at **www.PracticalBliss.com** or via email at **Lisa@Practicalbliss.com** to schedule a complimentary coaching session to help guide you toward identifying your purpose. You can also check out www.thehappymovie.com for more examples of living on purpose, passion, and flow.

CHAPTER SIX

Stepping Off the Edge

"Fear is not real. It is the product of thoughts you create. Do not misunderstand me. Danger is very real. But fear is a choice."
–Will Smith

You've identified your purpose, your passion, and your character strengths. So now what? If I were coaching you live, I'd start to nudge you onto the part where I ask you to get really clear on what your vision or dream is *for your life*. It's not mandatory to take this guide further than simply adding more joy and meaning to your daily life, but since you've gone this far, why not think about expanding your efforts into the long- and short-term goals you want to achieve in your lifetime? In fact, you may want to take a few moments to start to envision, without allowing any doubts, fears, or specific strategies to fall into the mix. What would your ideal life look like if you could create any outcome you wanted? Would you start your own business, travel to someplace you've always wanted to go, learn a new language, go part-time in your career, or maybe downsize your home and invest in a vacation spot, begin a new relationship . . . or something else altogether? Come on, let's explore your options. This'll be fun!

Try this: Find a quiet spot where you won't be interrupted and grab a pen. For the next ten to fifteen minutes (or more), turn off the phone, shut down email, and go off the grid. Remember the exercise we did in Chapter 4, where you imagined yourself on your very best day? Consider revisiting that spot, or maybe another spot all together—a place where you feel you're reaching your highest goals, maybe doing something you were born to do, or simply living each day with a balance of purpose, engagement, and pure pleasure. Remember that doubts, fears, and strategies have no place in this exercise—this is simply about identifying and recording what you really want to accomplish in this lifetime. Don't worry about making your vision perfect, or figuring out how you're going to get there. Just expand your vision and capture as many additional details as you can (how you look and feel, what you're doing, where you are, who's with you, where you live, etc.) without overthinking the exercise.

_____

_____

_____

_____

_____

_____

So how'd it go? Were you able to visualize one or two things? Or did you find it difficult to focus purely on the vision without letting fear of failure or doubts jump in on your dream? Did you jump right to the "how" before you allowed the "what" to take over your mind?

If so, I wouldn't be surprised. As humans, we're preprogrammed to lean toward the negativity bias,[47] as our early ancestors relied on it to detect danger and aid in survival. The doubts and fears we may have when we start to think of creating something more, different, or better than we currently experience is our internal protection device warning us to consider the ramifications of our actions. This can be useful—if we teach ourselves to manage the thoughts and feelings effectively. In fact, these thoughts and feelings will *assist you* in clarifying where you may need to develop strategies and solutions to enable success.

The Fear of Happiness

Pure pleasure can be frightening. I'm not talking about the kind of fear that keeps us from approaching, like fear of a haunted house brimming with zombies wielding chainsaws and machetes. I'm talking about the kind of fear that makes us curious, giddy, and a little nervous, as if we're doing something that's outside the zone of safety.

Whenever I'm in a place of pure pleasure, that feeling bubbles up almost unexpectedly and takes my breath away—like standing too close to the edge of the Grand Canyon. I'm in awe of the beauty, the rarified air, how far I've come, but all too aware of how far the fall would be should I indulge by closing my eyes and stepping a bit too far over the edge.

It's so much easier to avoid the feeling all together. After all, when we're cynical and "realistic" (as I've heard so many well-intending people say), we can avoid the danger by managing (and even lowering) our expectations and

---

[47] "Our Brain's Negative Bias | Psychology Today," 2009, https://www.psychologytoday.com/articles/200306/our-brains-negative-bias (accessed March 10, 2016).

negotiating down our dreams so that we simply can't be hurt or disappointed. If we don't play now, then we won't have to pay later. Makes sense. Especially when the message has been ingrained into our psyche since the dawn of time.

"The intention that man should be happy is not in the plan of creation."

"We are never so defenseless against suffering as when we love."

"The madman is a dreamer awake."

–Sigmund Freud

Entire cultures are built around the belief that happiness is an indulgence—and certainly shouldn't be flaunted, as it might create envy in others. The Japanese and Swiss are just two cultures with this deeply engrained idea. Could that be why so many of us convince ourselves to step away from the threshold within moments of our arrival at the door to happiness? Could we actually be denying ourselves bliss because we're afraid of what might happen when we lose it again—or what others might think of us if we dare to reach for something more, different, or even better than our current reality?

There are likely many reasons why we hold back from running full steam ahead toward joy, fun, excitement, and, perhaps especially, our dreams. However, before I move into some of the more common reasons, let's take a moment to talk about *you*. You are, after all, the reason that this book exists. Let's make this personal.

When you think about shifting your life around in order to include more purpose, more engagement, and more pleasure, I'm willing to bet you have a few reasons for believing (and perhaps even insisting) that incorporating these elements isn't something you can achieve. I get it, and the odds are that I've either experienced similar resistance myself or heard it from my clients, friends, or colleagues at one time or another. But I've found that it can be very helpful to purge all that noise and doubt from our heads by putting it onto paper, where we can start to sort through the tidbits of information.

EXERCISE - PURGING YOUR CLOSET

In this exercise you're going to make a list of every possible thing that may stop you from going after the vision you have for your life.

YOU WILL NEED:

Paper and pen or computer
Timer

Directions: Set a timer for two minutes and forty-five seconds. Once you've started the timer, quickly list (using the space below) every possible doubt, fear or current reality that stands between you and your ideal life. Be sure to consider all areas, including your personal, professional, physical, financial and relational situations, as well as any other area of your life that you can think of.

Tip: Don't waste time judging yourself during or after this exercise. Think of it as simply purging your closet and laying everything out to take a look. When you're finished, we'll start sorting and sifting through what we find.

Examples:
My job is too stressful.
I don't have enough time.
Happiness doesn't last (and I don't want to disappoint myself later).

EXERCISE - NAME THAT THEME

Look at your list and see where you can start to identify themes. I've listed some of the most common themes below. If you feel your examples fall under any of these themes, list them under that column. You can also add your own themes.

THEME	NOT ENOUGH TIME	NOT ENOUGH MONEY	I SHOULD BE DOING SOMETHING ELSE	IT WONT LAST	I'M NOT ENOUGHT (TOO SHORT, TALL, YOUNG, OLD, ETC.)	THERE'S NO SECURITY	FEAR OF FAILURE
Example	Work is crazy right now	I need to get my finances in order!	My kids need my full attention	I can't be disappointed again	I need to lose 5 lb. first	I can't leave my long-term career	What if I fall on my face?

Were you able to identify the themes in your list? I first completed a similar exercise in 2006, when I was contemplating (or rather, agonizing over) starting my own business. I had a list of about fifty reasons why I couldn't possibly think about leaving the security of my salaried twenty-year career. But when I sorted through the reasons, I realized they all boiled down to the themes listed in the exercise. Not coincidentally, I've noticed that when my clients complete this exercise, they too find that their issues fall into similar themes.

Because it's more than likely that these issues are causing you to consciously or subconsciously avoid achieving your bliss, it's important to face them head-on. With that in mind, let's look at some of the most common themes listed here (in no particular order).

1. I should be doing something else
2. It won't last
3. There's not enough money
4. There's not enough time
5. Fear of failure

Theme 1: If I Could Save Thyme in a Bottle

I can't tell you how many times I've worked to get to a point where I can relax . . . And *just* when I get there, I convince myself that it's time to get back to work! Is it just me, or can you relate?

I remember one of my clients telling me that she was having trouble finding time to really relax and enjoy her family. So I asked her to tell me about her last day off with them. She told me that her son, who was about thirteen years old, asked her to go swimming with him (which was rapidly becoming a rare treat, as anyone who's been in close proximity to a teenager knows). It was a beautiful day, and they were splashing and laughing and having fun in the pool. He was talking about his friends and something funny that had happened the day before. Suddenly she looked up at the clock (by the way, don't ever put a clock out by your pool), and realized that it was getting late in the afternoon and that she *needed* to jump out of the pool to squeeze in a trip to the grocery store so she could buy thyme . . . in a bottle, for a recipe. Mind you, she wasn't having dinner guests and there were no requirements that she made that particular recipe that evening. And yet in that moment she had it in her mind that she just had to get to the grocery store.

Seriously, can you see the irony here? Would the world have stopped if she neglected to purchase that seasoning? Yet how many times do we *pull* ourselves away from the **very thing** we say we want more of . . . only to do something we really need to do less of? When we talked about that, she told me she couldn't think of one single emergency that would *ever* occur in the event that she didn't have thyme on hand.

I suspect that this has happened to all of us, at one time or another. Even though you and I may *know* that some things aren't truly mandatory, we can still fall prey to social pressure and shy away from free time and fun in order to stick to the hectic, harried lifestyle that plagues so many over-achieving, successful men and women. The hectic, harried lifestyle that we've actually created for ourselves, because we *think* we need to for one reason or another, and then force ourselves to continue.

But when does the hurry-scurry rat racing end? When have you given up enough of your precious time, memories, and relationships to hold your head up and say "enough"? When will we have the courage to make that stand? Are you brave enough to admit to yourself, and others, that you *deserve* to be truly happy? Beyond that, are you brave enough to admit when you actually *are* happy? It seems like it's almost taboo to say it aloud, as if we need to pay penance for uttering the word lest the gods wreak revenge upon us. So we fall into the trap that leads us to believe that we *should* be doing something other than enjoying ourselves.

But life is too short. You *should* be creating and experiencing every enjoyable moment. That's what the point of achieving bliss is all about—if only we can get ourselves to "indulge" in the rewards of our efforts!

Theme 2: The Honeymoon's Over

Aside from the social stigma of declaring that we're happy, there's also, for me at least, the fear that if I allow myself to become too happy and engaged when I'm riding high, it will hurt like hell when I fall to the ground. Which brings us back to why so many of us negotiate our hopes and dreams down to very small, easily managed, low-risk endeavors that will allow us to carefully go about our days until we ultimately arrive safely at our death.

So let's see if we can't shed some new light on the topic of happiness and pure pleasure.

I've talked about "bliss" throughout this book, defining it as being the intersection where purpose and engagement meet pleasure. And while ultimate bliss may require these three components to actualize itself, happiness does not.

The question, of course, is what the difference could possibly be. And the second question you're probably asking yourself right now is this: If I could have happiness, and it's easier than having bliss, then why wouldn't I just stop there? The answer is simple: If you can have all-out bliss, then why stop at happiness, which is just the first step?

Let me explain. I mentioned earlier that I've found pure pleasure to be pretty scary. At least I did, until I realized there's a difference between happiness and pure pleasure. When you're living your life in alignment with your purpose and passion, happiness becomes a set point that isn't dependent on the positive feeling or experience that happens *to you in any given moment.* In other words, happiness is a fixed state, whereas pure pleasure (fun, peace, joy, excitement, etc.) will fluctuate—often moment by moment.

Pleasure can be fleeting. But a state of happiness is constant. *If* you're living the right sort of life.

If we can get away from being attached to thinking that a positive feeling or experience will keep us feeling happy, and just enjoy the moment without fear of losing our happiness when that positive experience subsides, the fear ceases to exist.

Take a look at the image below. Notice that when you combine general happiness with a positive feeling or experience, you may culminate *pure pleasure.* That moment that takes your breath away and is so unbelievably joyous (or peaceful, or exciting, or interesting) isn't to be feared for risk of losing it, because we already accept that it's fleeting. It's to be savored and fully enjoyed!

When I was on my honeymoon, I was having the most

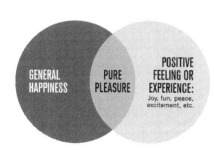

amazing time in one of the most beautiful places I'd ever seen. However, the closer I got to returning home, the more anxious I found myself becoming. I was afraid I would never experience that same level of pure pleasure again. By the time I returned home, it wasn't good—I was starting to slip into a funk and had to turn to one of my coaches to sort through the feelings. Why in the world was I feeling so down when I had just experienced my dream wedding and honeymoon? What was *wrong* with me?

What I realized is that it was true—I most likely would never experience that *exact same* feeling of pure pleasure again. But just because the honeymoon was over, it didn't mean the happiness had to fade as I returned to my everyday life. There would be a million other pleasures in the coming days, years, and months, and they would all add to the consistent feeling of happiness that I was building. Those pleasurable moments were just the building blocks. The pieces, not the whole.

Whether you've endured a moment with a nasty boss, lost a client, or failed to get the promotion, crappy things may happen. And yet it's entirely possible to continue to be a happy person—even in the midst of these moments. On the flip side, amazing things may happen that shift you into a state of pure pleasure, and then subside. That doesn't mean your overall happiness disappears once they're over.

In fact, research shows us that by simply *thinking* about past experiences, and feeling gratitude, we boost endorphins and contribute to our enduring happiness.

True happiness isn't dependent upon the Universe finding favor and shining down upon us. The Universe doesn't care either way—it's not out to get us, and it doesn't have a particular favor toward us. *It's up to us to decide we're going to be happy*, even when we don't get the job, the relationship doesn't work out, we haven't lost those last ten pounds, etc. We can accept and move on, setting ourselves up to embrace the next pleasurable moment.

When you're truly happy, it's almost as if you have a diversified portfolio. Meaning that if and when one of your investments ceases to be available (or profitable), it doesn't mean you're going to jump out of the nearest window! You're going to look at your entire portfolio and see where you can make up the difference with one of your other "investments," keeping your eyes wide open to find new opportunities!

Theme 3: Check the Water in the Pool Before You Jump

Since we're talking about portfolios and investments, it seems an appropriate time to bring up the doubts, fears, and concerns around current and future financial security. These are things that many people find to be keeping them from really finding bliss.

Helen Von Dolteren-Fournier,[48] certified financial planner and practicing attorney, works with her clients to put the plans in place to support just about any lifestyle or dream they can think of. Helen shares,

A lot of people spend more time planning their vacations than they spend planning what their retirement will look like. You can dream about what your future looks like and work with a CFP to make sure you have everything in place to make your dreams come true.

In fact, I first met Helen when I was only twenty-six years old and had absolutely no idea how much I would come to depend on our planning together to fund my dreams. I can tell you firsthand how important it's been for me to have an objective, well-developed short-and long-term financial plan that keeps me focused on developing my business rather than worrying about my financial future.

Additionally, keeping an eye on planning for your financial future extends to more than just funding your larger

---

[48] Helen Von Dolteren-Fournier, J.D., SPHR, CFP®, is a certified financial planner and practicing attorney. She is president of Aegis Advisors and offers a full suite of financial planning solutions with a holistic approach to helping you make your dreams come true. http://www.aegis-rj.com/

dreams. It also plays a key role in helping you bring more joy and meaning into your daily life.

Helen goes on to say,

According to the NY Times, couples who disagree about finances just once a week are more than 30 percent more likely to get divorced. That means that ensuring that you and your significant other have the same vision for your future is essential in maintaining your marital bliss!

She also reminds us that "When you feel good about your finances, you can focus on doing more good in this life—and bliss will follow." And as research shows us, " . . . people who help others usually have healthier, happier lives."[49]

If you really want to feel authentic bliss, take care of clearing up any debt, financial planning, insurance, setting up your will, etc. and see if you don't find yourself able to breathe more freely.

Theme 4: Never Enough Hours in the Day

I'm sure I've uttered those words before, and I'm fairly sure you may have too. With all you have going on every single day, how in the world are you supposed to carve out time to do anything else?

Good question. A few years ago, it occurred to me that the *one thing* that is equally distributed to each and every one of us is time. From Steve Jobs, to Mother Theresa, to you and me, we all have access to the exact same number of seconds, minutes, and hours in a day. It's how we decide to distribute them that makes the difference.

---

[49]Post, Stephen G. "Altruism, happiness, and health: It's good to be good." *International journal of behavioral medicine* 12.2 (2005): 66-77.

I like to think of the concept of time as if it were a bank balance, with the option to use every second to either invest in your future or frivolously spend with no expected return. You can make deposits by investing your time in meaningful projects, education, relationship building, improving your health, and anything else that may bring you a "return." *Or* you can spend your time on the optional obligations and stressors that bring you down, wear you out, and have little or nothing to do with the intention/vision you have for your life. In that case, you're not banking anything. You're frittering away your time without investing it, and at the end of the page, you don't have an equal return.

Let me backtrack for a moment because I suspect you might have gotten a little hung up on the words *"optional obligations and stressors"*—am I right?

After personally and professionally coaching people for more than fifteen years, I've noticed that most of us tend to commit to some things in our lives that we are neither passionate about nor truly *required* to do. I'm talking about those things like going to lunch with a negative co-worker, agreeing to be on a committee you could care less about, constantly cleaning up after and waiting on family, friends, and co-workers who are entirely capable of doing things for themselves, etc. Any of those stressors sound familiar to you?

When it comes to Living in Bliss, you're going to need to find room in your days, weeks, and months to include the events and things that truly make you feel good, and weed out the stuff that doesn't. So let's get started!

EXERCISE WEEDING OUT THE WASTE

Step 1: Make a list of the enjoyable and/or meaningful activites you currently like/love about your personal and professional life.

Step 2: List primary and routine tasks and responsibilities from your typical day/week, both personal and professional (list both enjoyable and stressful).

Step 3: List enjoyable and/or meaningful activities you **want to add** to your personal and professional life (daily and periodic)

Step 4: Transfer the tasks listed (above) to the appropriate boxes in the diagram below. Example: If giving presentations is something you love to do and it's mandatory, it belongs in the upper left box.

If having lunch with a negative co-worker is something that stresses you out and is not truly REQUIRED, it belongs in the bottom right box.

LOVE IT/ PRODUCTIVE

STRESSES ME OUT!

Giving presentations at work Leading a team through a successful project Raising my child	Wine tasting with friends Making cookies with the kids Getting up early to have breakfast w/my teenager before school
Creating endless reports Mowing the lawn Making dinner every night	Lunch with crabby co-worker Doing all the housework on my own

MANDATORY **OPTIONAL**

LOVE IT/ PRODUCTIVE

STRESSES ME OUT!

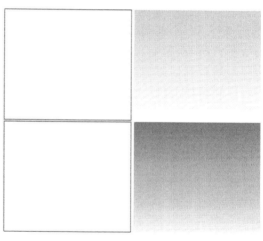

MANDATORY **OPTIONAL**

*Note: All items in the bottom right box (Optional Stress) can and *should* be weeded from your daily routine!

A word of caution here: When I've led clients through this exercise, they often have a hard time identifying tasks to put in the optional stress box. Yup, I've even fallen into that trap myself. That's because what *appears* to be mandatory can oftentimes actually be an *optional task in disguise.* That said, be very careful here! Just because your co-worker or boss (as was the case for me many years ago) assumes you're going to join them for an incredibly stressful, negative, and anything-but-relaxing lunch each day, *it doesn't mean it's mandatory.* In fact, when I realized that it might be time for me to find alternative lunch dates at work, I began building relationships that ultimately led to a promotion that kick started my entire career. **One tip on this:** Make sure that when you decide to say "No" where you need to, you do it in a firm yet tactful way so as not to burn any bridges as you go. I learned that lesson the hard way.

To summarize the tasks you've placed in the bottom right box: You know **all that crap you hate doing, that isn't all that important, anyway?** Stop doing it! There, I've said it, and it's a good thing I did. Because I can say with a staggering amount of accuracy that no one else will tell you to stop doing the things you don't *need* to be doing, *even if it's killing you.* You're welcome. If you feel you might benefit from some assistance in this area, go to my website at www.PracticalBliss.com and contact me to set up your complimentary coaching session.

Now go invest the time you gained in doing things in your optional/love it box (aka, the goodie box)!

The Goodie Box

Yes, that's the sweet spot you're dreaming of yet probably aren't experiencing as often as you'd like. I'm talking about the upper right box—the stuff that lights you up, yet is optional—also known as the stuff that gets the axe when you feel the consistent need to be selfless. I've said this before and I'm sure I'll say it again—when you're constantly in selfless/martyr mode, you're not doing anyone any favors. Think about it—when we continuously sacrifice the feeling of joy, satisfaction, and self-worth that comes from doing things we love to do (both personally and professionally), some of the first emotions to follow are bitterness, exhaustion, and resentment. None of which translates into bliss for anyone. It's in *everyone's* best interest that you take care of your physical and emotional needs consistently, so that you're sustainable for everyone who depends on you!

Dealing with the Inevitable—the Bottom Left Box
(responsibilities that are mandatory and stressful)

We all have mandatory stressors, or things that absolutely must get done. It's just a part of our lives. Sometimes we enjoy the stressor (example: caring for an infant), and sometimes we don't (example: maintaining the lawn, hedges, etc.).

Knowing that these things can't be avoided without creating additional stress, it's important that we develop a strategic plan for dealing with each mandatory task and responsibility without harming our own happiness.

Practical Tips for Managing Mandatory Stress

1) Make sure the stress is *truly mandatory*. Use the weeding-out exercise to verify your category. Note—if the consequences of eliminating these tasks **are not detrimental**, then they are not truly mandatory. Example: not caring for an infant or completing mandated projects at work *would be* detrimental. Not volunteering for the next fundraiser likely *wouldn't* be detrimental.

2) Prioritize. I know—all the stuff that's mandatory is already at the top of your list. Try this: Sort by **what can't wait** rather than sorting by what's important (example: sending a check to the IRS by a certain date can't wait, whereas submitting your expense report may be able to fall in priority below the IRS task).

3) Make friends with people outside your work environment and/or family. And ask for their point of view. Sometimes it's just easier to talk to someone who isn't so close to the action. It allows you to gain a new perspective, practical tips, and ability to voice how you really feel. This is one of the many reasons people choose to engage in a coaching relationship.

4) Stay away from people *who are more stressed than you.* I can't stress this enough because I've fallen into this bottomless pit myself. At first if feels good to feel like maybe you have your stuff together enough to be able to lift someone else up. If, however, that person relies on stress and drama as their default state *every day*, run as fast as you can, because that energy will slowly consume you and leave you feeling like a used and worn-out old shoe.

5) Look for personal and professional mentors. Go out of your way to make connections with positive, successful people who exude the kind of fun-loving, joy-seeking energy you're looking for! Go to www.InBlissLife.com/community to connect with great people like you!

6) Keep in mind that perfection seldom leads to bliss. Give it your best and move on! Enough said.

7) Slow your roll. Did you know it takes roughly the same amount of time to frantically walk from one place to the next as is does to take long, graceful strides while breathing slowly along the way? Yup, no lie. As a bonus, you will be seen as a successful person who's got it all together rather than a frenzied person just trying to make it through another day! You can read more about this topic by going to http://inblisslife.com/bits/slow-your-roll.

Sending Out an SOS! (Stressors, Opinions, and Strategies)

We're smart people, and can generally come up with great plans to help our employees, co-workers, clients, spouses, kids, and friends out when they need it, right? So let's take a few minutes to come up with a solid plan for productively dealing with the mandatory stress for *ourselves*.

S.O.S. (Stressors, Opinions and Strategies) Examples

We can deal with the majority of our mandatory stress by either developing a strategic plan or changing our opinions about how and who can deal with the issues. Not surprisingly, many of our stressors take both a change in our core belief/opinion *and* a strategy to create a solid action plan. Use the exercise below to determine how to best deal with the responsibilities that stress you out and rob you of everyday bliss.

First: Determine whether your mandatory stress (found in the bottom left quadrant of the Weeding Out the Waste exercise) is either an opinion you've formed, something in need of a solid strategy, or both. See below for examples, and then use the spaces below that to decide how best to deal with your stress points.

STRESSOR:	OPINION? OR	STRATEGY?
(List the Stressor)	(is this just an opinion you've formed?)	(is there a strategy that needs to be developed?)
NEW OPINION AND/OR STRATEGY:	(what is your <u>new</u> opinion?)	(what can be done to lighten your load?)

EXAMPLES:

For the first stressor: Let's say you have a new puppy who's super cute and is also a complete terror! (Yes, I can relate to this one, and it's a good thing that puppy was cute!) First, let's decide whether his being a terror is something that just requires you adopt a new opinion, or something that requires a strategy. Maybe it's a combination of both.

The truth is, the dog is a terror. Yet it might be helpful to remember that he won't be a puppy forever (shift your opinion). Additionally, you can develop a few strategies to help you get through the puppy phase. See what I mean?

STRESSOR:	OPINION? OR	STRATEGY?
New puppy is a terror!!	X Yes, it's your opinion because it's true!	X Yes, needs strategy
NEW OPINION AND/OR STRATEGY:	He *is* pretty cute, and he won't be a puppy forever.	• Obedience training • Dog sitter • Buy a crate

EXERCISE - S.O.S.

For the second stressor: Kids need to be fed. Is that just a belief or does it require a strategy (or both)?

Do you believe the kids really need to be fed? Yes, I hope so. But, you may be able to shift your opinion that every meal needs to be provided by you and made from scratch. It's possible that you could develop a strategy to help you enlist other ways of getting the kids fed each day.

STRESSOR:	OPINION? OR	STRATEGY?
Kids need to be fed	X They really need to be fed, but every meal doesn't need to be made from scratch, by me	X Yes, needs a strategy
NEW OPINION AND/OR STRATEGY:	• I don't have to do it all myself • Sometimes it's OK to stop for fast food • It's time to teach my kids a few recipes!	• Stop for quick/healthy fast food • Make meals ahead of time and freeze • Teach older children to cook • Hire a meal delivery service a few nights/week

Ok, your turn to create your new action plan, using the template below. Remember, first determine whether the stressor is just a belief or if it could benefit from an action plan (or both). Next, include what the new belief could be, and lastly, include what steps you could include in your strategy.

FILL IN YOUR S.O.S.

STRESSOR:	OPINION? OR	STRATEGY?
NEW OPINION AND/OR STRATEGY:		

STRESSOR:	OPINION? OR	STRATEGY?
NEW OPINION AND/OR STRATEGY:		

As you can see, there are ways you may be able to manage some of the mandatory stress, like yard maintenance, childcare, and creating endless reports at work. In doing so, you can make yourself available for the mandatory stressors that truly require every bit of your attention to plan and carry out.

I remember when I first started my business (and had also become newly single around the same time). I decided I would maintain my lawn in order to cut the additional expense from my budget. After about the fourth week of straining to push my self-propelled mower up the hill in my front yard, though, and spending about three hours a week on the effort (sweating so much I *actually ruined the cell phone I had tucked into my sports bra!),* I decided that investing the $110 per month to hire a service was a very wise use of my income and resources. Additionally, I was able to utilize those three hours a week by putting the time toward marketing my business. A wise strategy I've never once regretted. I sat down and determined whether this was a mandatory stress, and how I could cope with it. And I made the move.

Enough Is Enough

I know that since you're a busy person who seeks more joy and meaning, it probably means that you also have a very busy life. So let's talk about how to deal with stress in your professional life, specifically. Early on in this book, I told you about the moment I realized that I was not Living in Bliss. I also realized that, for the most part, I had subconsciously created this scenario by overbooking my schedule, eliminating lunch breaks, and not allowing myself sufficient time between meetings. The truth is, there were definitely times when I could and should have been more savvy with my time and efforts—but my ego laughed off the suggestion.

Let me explain. During the years I've invested in both my corporate career and consulting and executive coaching in companies in various industries, I've come to notice a pattern that falls across all industry. That pattern is the idea that we need to be *busy* in order to be valuable to others (and even to ourselves).

I worked with a woman for eighteen years, we'll call her Janice, who never missed an opportunity to dramatically tell everyone around her how busy she was (at work and at home). She would walk very quickly wherever she went, constantly wringing her hands and appearing frazzled and drained. My impression was that she was working pretty hard to convey her value to anyone who would listen.

However, in most reputable companies, employers *don't want* their employees (particularly their leadership team) to work themselves into the ground. In fact, as a former executive myself, I much prefer employees who get the job done as efficiently and quickly as possible—leaving them physically and mentally energized for the next project.

But for some reason, many people equate being "busy" with being invaluable. It's not necessary to tell everyone how busy you are (how can you possibly take on more responsibility if that's the case?), but it *is* necessary to deliver results. Don't confuse the two! I wish someone had given me this tip before I spent half a decade figuring it out!

If you're feeling overwhelmed by your schedule and responsibilities, check in with yourself and use the above exercises. Are there meetings you may not really need to attend? Reports or tasks you may be able to delegate or automate? Are you trudging through the weeds rather than stepping back and being strategic about where you focus your efforts? If so, it's time to revisit your purpose, your passion, and the intention you have for your life. Using these components as a filter for how you invest or spend your time and energy may bring you more bliss than you know what to do with!

I encourage you to visit my professional development website at www.ActualizeResults.com for more tips, articles, and videos to help you develop your career in alignment with your life's vision.

Growth, Death, and Dignity

Why is it that just thinking or hearing the word "failure" can stop us in our tracks? In fact, I'm finding that just writing these words instantly reminds me of doubts, fears, and past failures I have lurking in the recesses of my mind.

The truth is that we all have fears and failures—*all of us*—both personal and professional, "unless we have no connection or empathy," according to Brené Brown, a leading expert on the topic of shame and vulnerability. We've all heard that we're supposed to look at our failures as a gift or a lesson and that "if we're not failing, we're not trying hard enough." Well in that case I must be trying pretty hard, because I've failed pretty often if you ask me—and sometimes felt a loss of my dignity and the pain of shame in the process.

Yes, failing can be a pretty emotionally challenging and painful endeavor, even inciting post-traumatic stress as an extra bonus. I won't pretend that it isn't an obstacle for me or anyone I know, because it certainly can be. However, I do believe that I've learned lessons and gained strengths from all of my past failures, and knowing that has kept me more open in the moment (or shortly thereafter).

Carin Rockind reminds us, " . . . we can *decide* to experience post-traumatic growth, which happens *at the same time* as post-traumatic stress, and *not instead of.*"[50] By processing the pain, shame, or trauma, in addition to understanding the lessons learned and gifts gained, you may be able to boost your resilience and bounce back faster from the situation.

Our failures and traumas can change us, that's true. They also provide us with opportunities to utilize the parts of ourselves that can spring into action when we need to protect ourselves. If you've ever heard someone say, "I had no idea I could be so quick, strong, brave, insightful . . ." then you know what I'm talking about. Once you've accessed those parts of yourself that benefit you, you're more easily able to access and utilize those strengths when you *aren't* facing failure, shame, or pain.

Take a look at the next image, which maps out the process of identifying 1) who you are at your core/your character, 2) the trauma or failure you experienced, 3) the resulting feeling you experienced, 4) the deep-rooted parts of you that sprang to life to help you cope and protect yourself from having it happen again, 5) what you gained as a result of utilizing these newly discovered parts of your character, and 6) what's left to process as a result of the incident.

---

[50] Calhoun, L. G., & Tedeschi, R. G. (1998). Posttraumatic growth: Future directions. In R. G. Tedeschi, C. L. Park, & L. G. Calhoun (Eds.), *Posttraumatic growth: Positive change in the aftermath of crisis* (pp. 215–238). Mahwah, NJ: Lawrence Erlbaum Associates, Inc.

Concentric circles diagram (from outer to inner):

WHAT'S LEFT TO PROCESS? PAIN, HURT, ANGER, ETC.

WHAT YOU'VE GAINED AS A RESULT OF THE BEHAVIORS: SUCCESS, SENSE OF HUMOR, KNOWLEDGE, HEALTHY BODY, ETC.

PERSONAL PROTECTION DEVICES: HUMOR, PERFECTION, DENIAL, WITHDRAWAL, WARRIOR, ETC.

RESULTING FEELINGS: SHAME, FEAR, GUILT, LOSS, ETC.

TRAUMA: DIVORCE, CAR ACCIDENT, LOSS OF JOB

YOUR CHARACTER/ ESSENCE:

EX: Creative and compassionate

CIRCLE OF EXPERIENCE EXAMPLES:

Trauma: Divorce, car accident, job loss, violence
Resulting Feelings: Shame, fear, guilt, loss, etc.
Personal Protection: Humor, perfection, denial, withdrawl, warrior, etc.
What You Gained As a Result: Success, sense of humor, knowledge, new skills, etc.
What's Left to Process: Pain, hurt, overactive perfectionist, anger, etc.

114

Exercise - Circle of Experience

Think about the last failure you experienced, the feeling you had, the part of you that acted as your protector, and what you gained as a result. Use the next image to chart your experience.

WHAT'S LEFT TO PROCESS?

WHAT YOU'VE GAINED AS A RESULT OF THE BEHAVIORS:

PERSONAL PROTECTION DEVICES:

RESULTING FEELINGS:

TRAUMA:

YOUR CHARACTER/
ESSENCE

Use this exercise to help ground yourself the next time you "fail," and see if it doesn't help you stand up and dust yourself off with dignity. Because it's true—if you're not failing you're not learning, and that's a gift you don't want to miss out on.

Now use this space to jot down notes and wisdom points you've gained in this chapter:

_____

_____

_____

_____

_____

_____

_____

_____

_____

CHAPTER SEVEN

Making It Stick!

"Your assumptions are your windows on the world. Scrub them off every once in a while, or the light won't come in." —Isaac Asimov

"A mind is like a parachute. It doesn't work if it is not open."
—Frank Zappa

At this point in our journey together, you've done some great work; you've explored your purpose, rediscovered or uncovered new passions, faced your fears, opened the door to reassess your priorities, and looked at ways to create more time to truly engage in your life. Congratulations—you're well on your way!

That being said, I think we both know it would be naive for us to believe that you're going to easily integrate everything we've discussed into your life the first time you try. You're going to need a little support to really create lasting changes in your life. Believe me, I know this better than most because it certainly took some time for me to get the hang of it. In this chapter, we'll look at the thoughts, feelings, and actions that may help to ensure that your efforts stick around for the long haul.

A Born Critic

Growing up, I wasn't a particularly positive person. In fact, from a very early age, I distinctly remember an ongoing practice where I would sit on the couch with my family, watching TV and spewing out an endless supply of critique at the actors, actresses, and commercials that appeared on the screen. This would ultimately culminate with my dad finally having heard enough and pointing out to me that no one was paying me to be a critic and that I should keep my comments to myself. Unfortunately, I regarded his advice as more of a suggestion than a directive.

This went on well into my twenties and thirties, as this practice had become a regular way of life for me. I had worked in the entertainment field for more than fifteen years (a cynical environment in its own right) and at that point I *was* in fact being paid (in part) to give my critique. My mom took great delight in reminding my dad of this often.

Needless to say, I wasn't a very blissful person in general. I'm sure I alienated friends and irritated my co-workers and employees, and I could honestly describe myself as exhausting. Sure, it was kind of fun to riff for a while with some of my entertainment industry co-workers (usually at the expense of someone or something else), but by the end of each day I felt worn out, depressed, and incredibly remorseful.

Thankfully, when I was about thirty-six years old and an entertainment manager, our department underwent some changes and a new vice president came in to lead us. Our new VP was unlike any we had ever had in the past, and took an entirely different approach to our industry and life in general. He had innovative new ideas and invested time in getting to know each person on his management team, so he could understand our strengths and challenges. After months of asking my opinion about costumes, sets, and show and event concepts, he gave me an incredible gift that changed my life in many ways.

At the end of one of my ongoing commentaries about what I thought was wrong with whatever the topic was (which by this point I'm sure had expanded to current events and people in general), he politely stopped me and asked if I wouldn't mind hearing a suggestion he had. Given that I was his direct report, naturally I accepted the offer.

He then very tactfully but firmly told me that he felt I had a solid grasp and was exceptionally gifted at being able to pinpoint and articulate what I believed to be wrong *in any given situation.* In fact, I was so gifted that he felt it was time to hone another, perhaps more valuable, talent to rival my gift. He suggested that I now look to see what I believed to be *right* about my surroundings and situations.

What? Who ever heard of such a thing? The whole idea of searching my surroundings to see what I liked in any given situation was completely foreign to me. I couldn't for the life of me see the benefit of conducting this experiment! But being the perfectionist that I was, I decided to give it my full effort.

So I did. Heeding his advice, I carried a little notebook around with me everywhere I went. My task was to step into every situation with a single focus: to identify and articulate at least three things I liked about the environment, culture, and/or situation.

At first I found it quite a challenge to set aside my old routine. Yet given the challenge to find not one but *three* positive elements went a long way toward keeping me occupied enough to help break my lifelong habits.

I began by looking for the obvious everywhere I went; did I like the color of the carpet on the floor or maybe the paint on the walls? Did I like the curtain fabric, or the taste of the food in a restaurant? Did I like the song that was playing in the background or the service someone provided? I kept a running list in my tiny notebook, to prove that I was making a solid go of it.

After a while, I began to challenge myself to pinpoint details I hadn't noted before. I started noticing people who committed random acts of kindness or smiled at each other. I noticed details about the sights, sounds, and experiences I encountered everywhere I went. I also noticed that I started applying this new approach to my relationships, searching to find what I liked about the people in my personal and professional life rather than what irritated and annoyed me about them. But the thing I noticed most of all was *how much better I felt* when I stopped looking for what was wrong and started focusing on what was right.

I know we've probably all heard the saying, "You can't teach an old dog new tricks," and up until that point in my life, I truly believed that we were who we were and there was no getting around it. For the first time in my life, though, I questioned my status quo … and I actually liked the genuinely positive person I was becoming. I wondered, was it really possible to reprogram ourselves to think and behave differently? And if so, would it stick for more than a few days?

The short answer to that question? Yes, you can change the way you think and behave, regardless of your age, if you *want* to do so. Thanks to what we now know about neuroplasticity[51] and the brain, scientists confirm that by consistently and deliberately changing your conscious thoughts and behaviors, and continuing to learn new information, over time you can actually change your brain's

---

[51]"Neuroplasticity," Wikipedia, 2011, https://en.wikipedia.org/wiki/Neuroplasticity (accessed March 11, 2016).

physical structure and functional organization to make the lasting changes you want to experience.

Why Change is Possible

As I mentioned earlier, our minds are prewired toward the negativity bias as a means to solve problems and survive–whether the situation includes an actual threat or not. That's due in part to the fact that "While the left brain understands and processes every word that we use, the right brain understands every word but one—the word *not*."[52] So while that combination is sometimes a helpful tool for avoiding actual danger or harm, it also sometimes hinders us by operating in overdrive when there's no need to be on the defensive. Knowing this now, I can only surmise that my brain must've thought there was plenty of reason to be on the defensive for a good portion of my earlier life and career! The problem is that when we're constantly on guard for anything that may pose a threat, it's very likely that happiness and bliss will remain far from our reach.

When you completed the Circle of Experience exercise in the last chapter, you identified how your negative experiences triggered your internal protection mechanisms and served you in terms of your overall success. Knowing that you've likely used those thoughts to your advantage in the past, you certainly don't want to insult yourself by condemning your instincts in the future. What you want to do instead is to identify *when* and *how* you can start to shift to more positive thoughts, beliefs, and behaviors in the future.

Since you're no doubt an intelligent and rational person, I'm going to assume that your behaviors are typically carried out as a result of the thoughts and beliefs you've formed

---

[52] Aldo R. Pucci, "Feel the Way You Want to Feel ... No Matter What!" New York: iUniverse, 2010.

throughout the course of your lifetime. This is both good news and bad. Let me explain.

From a very early age, you've been accumulating the collection of beliefs that you now hold about yourself, those around you, and the world in general. The thoughts and beliefs you've collected are likely formed by the experiences you've had in your environment and with your family, friends, and co-workers. Once you've repeated the thoughts over and over to yourself, the thought becomes a belief. And as Dr. Albert Ellis illustrates in the ABC Model,[53] your behavior and the resulting consequences are likely based on those beliefs.

Example:
A = Activating Event—The situation or event (ie, you can't find your car keys)
B = The Belief—The belief you have about that event and what it means (ie, you can't find your car keys and believe it will make you late for work, which means you may get fired)
C = The Consequence—The feelings and behaviors caused by our beliefs (ie, you freak out and condemn yourself and everyone around you because your life will be ruined as a result of misplacing your keys)

Obviously this is an exaggerated example, but you see how your mind can quickly jump to a conclusion that impairs your rational thinking (and actions). As a matter of fact, in my experience teaching conflict resolution across the nation, my participants have told me that looking back, they could easily see how they may have overreacted to a seemingly trivial event because of their past experience in an even remotely similar situation.

---

[53] "The ABC Method of Stress Reduction," 2012, http://www.dartmouth.edu/~eap/abcstress2.pdf (accessed March 12, 2016).

When the brain fears that it might be in danger, our fight or flight instinct kicks in and all bets are off. However, the more we learn about and work to grow our positivity, the more we can train our brains to control our responses and be more positive, which will in turn create more positive consequences and contribute to a more blissful existence.

As you may have guessed, that was a trick question. Both columns contain the exact same number of positive and negative words. However, your brain was probably in search of negativity, and understandably honed in on the negative words and the threat they represent.

Carin Rockind shares more on this, in regard to the Prospecting Theory:[54] " . . . Our brain processes a loss or threat as being more impactful than experiencing a gain. If we lost $20 on the street and afterwards we were handed a $20 bill, later on we'd still feel the loss stronger than the gain!" Which means we will instinctively hone in on what we assess to be a loss rather than a gain.

However, if you can start to consistently train your brain to look for the positive in each situation, speak more often of positive emotions and events, and surround yourself with positive people, your brain will start to get the message that things are going to be a little different around here.

Me, Myself, and I

Besides looking outside ourselves for more positive situations than negative, it's equally (if not perhaps more) important to take a look at the messages we're experiencing internally.

Remember, the right brain understands every word except the word "not." That means that when you hear or think things like "We do not have a problem" or "I'm not going to beat myself up about this" you may still find yourself becoming defensive or assuming something is going to go wrong or already is wrong. With that in mind, we have to program ourselves to start thinking a whole lot less about what *we do*

---

[54] Prospect theory." Wikipedia https://en.wikipedia.org/wiki/Prospect_theory (accessed April 25, 2016)

not want to do or *do not want,* and think a lot more about what we *do* want to *do* or want more of.

For example:

INSTEAD OF THIS:	THINK THIS
"I'm not going to beat myself up about this	"I'm going to go easy on myself and have more self-compassion about this."
"I'm not going to criticize all my flaws"	"I'm really proud of the way I'm taking care of myself."
"I'm not goint to be so stressed, frazzled, behind, busy, etc. anymore."	"I'm making time for the things that matter most to me."
	Or
	"I'm working to streamline my efforts, delegate more often, and leave time for me to take care of myself."

Remember, when you're constantly in the process of determining what's wrong, you'll stay in the process indefinitely. This isn't about over-inflating your ego and stepping on others to get ahead. It's about treating yourself with kindness, being mindful of the growth you're experiencing, and being cognizant of how you process and communicate daily occurrences. Is the glass half empty? You get where I'm going with this.

Over, Around, or Through

Ok, we've established the need to train your mind to look for the positive, awesome! That being said, I can almost hear you asking "But what about the times when I've legitimately hit a roadblock or failed at something I've tried?" I hear you, and I know how frustrating and painful those experiences can be. Unfortunately, it took a bit more time to silence my inner critic than it did to tune out the external critique.

When it comes to processing my roadblocks and failed attempts, I fully admit that in the past (and occasionally in the present) my first instinct is to approach the incident with a fixed and judgmental mindset, rather than viewing it as an opportunity for growth. Fortunately, over the years, I've found an incredibly good resource to help move my mindset from judging to learning.

Marilee Adams, PhD, founder of the Inquiry Institute,[55] shares that when we judge with questions such as "What's wrong with me? "Why bother?" or "Why are they so stupid?" we adopt a "fixed mindset" and trigger feelings of negativity, stress, and hopelessness. However, when we ask ourselves learning-based questions such as "What are the facts?" "What can I learn?" and "What's best to do now?" we create a "growth mindset" that triggers feelings of possibilities, understanding, and flexibility.

---

[55] "Inquiry Institute," 2007, http://inquiryinstitute.com/ (accessed March 14, 2016).

QUIZ - LEARNER OR JUDGER?

Take a look at the statements below and place a check mark in either the Agree **or** Disagree columns to select which of the statements sound **most like your instinctive response** to challenges and setbacks. C'mon, be honest with yourself.

	THOUGHT / STATEMENT	AGREE?	DISAGREE?
1	What's wrong with everyone around here?		
2	What assumptions am I making about this?		
3	I might need to ask more questions and gain more knowledge about the situation.		
4	If I were any good at my career, I'd already know the answer to this problem.		
5	What if I fail again? I can't take any more disappointment.		
6	It certainly isn't my fault.		
7	What are my options? What else can I do?		
8	This decision would be tough for anyone to make; what else do I need to consider?		
	Record the total points in each of the columns, using the scoring guide below.		

Scoring: Give yourself 2 points **each** for checking #2, 3, 7, or 8 in the **Agree** column. Write your total for the Agree column in the total box.

Give yourself 2 points **each** for checking #1, 4, 5, or 6 in the **Disagree** column. Write your total for the Disagree column in the total box.

Add the sum of points in the Agree and Disagree columns and record it here _____.

Results: If you scored between **0-12 points,** you may lean more towards the fixed/judger mindset.

If you scored between **13-16 points,** It you may lean towards a growth/learner mindset.

Visit www.inquiryinstitute.com to see an illustration of the Learner/Judger Path.

While knowing the difference between the two mindsets is important, it's only half the battle—as my husband reminded me one day when I received some critical feedback about my brand new, soon-to-be-launched website . . . and went spiraling full speed down the path of self-criticism and judgment.

When our instincts send us down the wrong path, it's important to be able to recognize what's going on and switch lanes as quickly as possible. That's why it can be really useful to share the concept of fixed and growth mindset with your family, friends, and peers—so that you can rely on each other to (gently) raise a flag when it looks like you're headed in the wrong direction. The quicker you self-correct, the quicker you bounce back from roadblocks and perceived failures.

Once I allowed myself to fully wallow in frustration and disappointment about the website feedback for a good half hour, I switched to a learner mindset and looked to see what improvements could be made. As a result, I am much happier with the design and the results that came out of the feedback.

When you are open to new ways of approaching the roadblocks to your success and happiness, you cease being a victim and create new ways of interacting with yourself and others. You may also be surprised to see how taking a learning and less defensive path can bring you more success in every area of your life. And how it can, ultimately, lead you toward achieving the quality of life you want to lead.

I'll Have What She's Having

While part of the process of making it stick is changing our reaction to setbacks and failures, and having a more positive outlook, another part of the process is avoiding the unconscious temptation to compare ourselves to others. Remember when we talked about self-compassion and "keeping your tape measure to yourself"? It's worth mentioning again here, because no matter what you do or accomplish, and no matter how much you practice self-care, your efforts will be essentially worthless if you aren't careful to avoid comparing yourself to others.

You know those times when you've caught a glimpse of yourself in the mirror and felt pretty good about what you saw … until you noticed someone else who appeared to be thinner, better dressed, have more hair, look more successful—you name it. I think you know what I mean.

Comparisons and jealousy are instinctive to humans, and even those who *aren't human* can feel jealousy, as Frans de Waal shares in his TED Talk,[56] *Capuchin Monkeys Reject Unequal Pay.* In his talk he shares video of his research, which features two monkeys who are both asked to hand the researcher a rock in exchange for a cucumber. Both monkeys deliver the rock and happily eat their cucumber payment. The next time the monkeys are asked to hand the researcher a rock, the first monkey is given a grape and the second monkey observes. The second monkey then delivers his rock and is handed a cucumber in return. Having seen the first monkey munching happily on his grape, the second monkey actually throws the cucumber back at the researcher and tries to snatch a grape in return!

Now that you know that jealousy is part of our natural instincts, don't beat yourself up for catching yourself in the act! The key is to set the criteria for what *you* believe is right for **you,** rather than using someone else's criteria for your life. I've

---

[56] "Capuchin monkeys reject unequal pay," YouTube, 2012, https://www.youtube.com/watch?v=gOtIN4pNArk (accessed March 14, 2016).

seen many of my clients and peers agonize over not reaching goals *they never really cared about obtaining in the first place.* Those goals belong to other people, and aren't necessarily better than the goals my clients and peers set for themselves—so why are they reacting that way? One reason: They're comparing themselves to others, and setting themselves up to fail in the process.

Additionally, remind yourself that you don't know what you don't know about the people you may see as "having it all." Though they may appear to have something you don't, *you* may have far more than they ever hope to gain. Which brings us to another key component in making it stick: gratitude.

Your Attitude About Gratitude

We've probably all heard how important it is to "look on the bright side" and have gratitude for the blessings in our life. I know I certainly have not only heard it, but have also reminded my clients to keep a sense of gratitude through everything they do. Nonetheless, I clearly remember sitting in my hammock, sobbing, just before Thanksgiving of 2009. I was feeling particularly irritated and low because I had been "thinking positively" for more than two years, and I *still* didn't have the thriving business and love life I wanted.

In fact, it really irritated me that I'd been helping my clients and friends get on board with the law of attraction[57] . . . and for what? So I could sit on the sidelines and cheer them on while I did without? How was this fair?! What did I have to be *thankful* for?

---

[57]"Law of attraction (New Thought)," Wikipedia, 2014, https://en.wikipedia.org/wiki/Law_of_attraction_(New_Thought) (accessed March 14, 2016).

Did I mention I was feeling particularly low?

When I reached the bottom of my pity party, I called my friend Karen, who invited me to stay the night with her and her family. I packed a bag and envisioned an evening of self-indulgence and sob stories abounding.

We did spend some time that evening drinking wine and lamenting and laughing about my run of gun-shy, would-be clients and dating fiascos. When I woke the next morning, I felt refreshed and ready to take on the world. Until I opened my email. The first message I saw was from my most promising client prospect, letting me know that her company had decided to wait until the next fiscal year to do the employee and leadership development we had planned to do.

Really?!! Why was I personally cursed to a life in limbo; waiting and waiting for this losing streak to turn around so I could start enjoying my life as an entrepreneur and newly single woman?

When Karen woke to make us breakfast, she found me huddled in a messy mass of streaked mascara and rumpled jammies. She let me unload for a bit … and then she didn't any more.

She straightened up, and told me to get dressed and to meet her in the kitchen to begin devising a plan for my next steps. Personally, my plan would've included a few days of moping and carb loading, but Karen didn't have that on her agenda. We spent the morning talking about my business strategy and how I might reach more client prospects and, perhaps more importantly, how critical it was to *truly* maintain an attitude of gratitude. In talking to Karen, I realized that although I had been telling my clients that very thing, I *personally* had become a little cynical about the subject and, at times, almost resentful.

She gave me three pieces of homework: 1) start a gratitude journal, 2) write about my "highest self," and 3) work on consistently fostering my business and relationship opportunities to increase my possibilities for success.

Feeling somewhat revived, I went home, pulled out my gratitude journal, and began to list everything in my life that I was grateful for in my current reality. At first, listing what I was grateful for wasn't easy. After all, I had taken a *huge* leap of faith and left my successful twenty-year career, then separated from my sixteen-year marriage, and refinanced my home—just before the economy crashed! Additionally, I had a ten-year-old boy who needed attention (and food, and clothes, and fun stuff), and no steady source of income!

In all honesty, at that time, I couldn't think of a single area of my life that was "settled" or inherently "blissful."

However, when I *really thought about it,* I had to admit that **in that moment, everything was fine**. In fact, none of the things I really worried about (losing my home and becoming a bag lady, dying alone and nobody noticing, etc.) had come to pass. I was holding my own with my household expenses, thanks in great part to Helen, my financial planner and encourager extraordinaire, and I had family and friends who loved and surrounded me.

I decided to follow the format I learned while studying the law of attraction (thoughts inspire action which begets "things"), and divided each journal page into two columns: what I'm grateful for now, and gratitude for what's on its way.

Looking back, there were times when I felt lonely and scared as I forced myself to capture my present gratitude list: the sun rising, a cool breeze, a roof over my head, my wonderful son, good health, the love of my long-time and new friends, a dependable car, etc. However, over time I began to realize that my gratitude was becoming more heart-felt and that this new routine was helping me reshape my days by way of the thoughts I nurtured and the actions I took. I would start each day with coffee on my back patio, where I would quietly sit and watch the sun rising over the trees, the water rippling on the surface of my tiny, deteriorating pool, and think about the possibility of creating a beautiful space out of my very overgrown and attention-starved yard. As I sat there, I consciously imagined the potential for what *could be* and reveled in my imaginary new surroundings. It was then that I noticed how much joy I felt when I was in that state, and I purposely lingered there before snapping back to my current reality. As I "came to," I would journal about what was "to be."

Ultimately I found that when I dove into capturing my gratitude for what was yet to be, I was moved and amazed at how easily the list seemed to write itself! It was as if my hand and pen were just the vehicles for expressing what was almost bursting at the seams to flow out of me. I wrote *"Love is looking for me, I just need to allow it to find me and accept it freely. It is beautiful and makes me laugh and takes my breath away. We dance and dine and talk deeply about things that move us in a positive way. We care about others and about joy and fun and freedom and passion … and so many other things I can't even begin to know. We help each other and others too. Our love is beautiful, warm, exciting, kind, fun, sweet, silly, serious, sexy and romantic. Life is good."*

I also wrote about my career and friendships. *"My business is thriving and success is all I know! It's a part of every piece of my life. My friendships are warm and beautiful, my business is bountiful, with clients who want to grow and learn! I love my work and I am free of worry and have wealth to spare. I am healthy in every way I want to be and my son is even better off. I love my life!"*

It was as if stripping away the layers of my picture postcard life left me raw and ready to reconstruct my existence in a way that was much more purposeful, deliberate, and discerning. I was no longer as concerned with *appearing as if* everything was perfect, and now much more focused on creating and appreciating real moments of joy, meaning, hope, and connection. In other words, I *decided* that I would purposely pursue bliss, and revel in every moment of it as if it were my last.

When my attitude began to really turn around, I began making a greater effort to put myself in situations where I would make it easier for success to find me.

As it turns out, I'm not alone in my experience. In fact, research shows[58] that "expressing gratitude increases your happiness by helping you notice the good things that are already happening." Additionally, gratitude has been shown to help us focus less on the negative, focus more on others, increase our optimism, and reduce our experience with the hedonic treadmill[59] by calling attention to areas where we're satisfied with our lives. That being said, let's take a look at what you're grateful for.

Putting It Into Practice

If you're reading this and thinking, "There's just no way I can find the time or energy to sit and contemplate my gratitude every morning or night," I hear you. In fact, there were many days then (and occasionally now) when I felt as if I were being frivolous with my time in spending five or ten

---

[58] Sheldon, Kennon M, and Sonja Lyubomirsky. "How to increase and sustain positive emotion: The effects of expressing gratitude and visualizing best possible selves." *The Journal of Positive Psychology* 1.2 (2006): 73-82.
[59] "Hedonic treadmill," Wikipedia, 2011, https://en.wikipedia.org/wiki/Hedonic_treadmill (accessed April 14, 2016).

minutes (or more) in my higher self and "gratitude of the future" world.

However, I recommend thinking about this exercise in another way. Instead of looking at it as time "spent," look at this as time "invested," the same way we talked about investing time as banking for the future. Even if you invest only five or ten minutes a day touching base with your "highest self" and envisioning your target life, you'll be reinforcing your beliefs and goals about who you are and how you want your life to be. In other words, you'll constantly have your target in view, which makes it much easier to know where to focus your efforts.

If you're struggling with where to squeeze the extra time into your already packed schedule, at this point all you need to do is *commit to* incorporating it into your routine because it's instrumental in creating the life you want to lead. Go back to the "Weeding Out the Waste" exercise in Chapter 6 to see which optional obligations and stressors can be replaced with completing this exercise a few times a week.

The important thing to keep in mind is that **gratitude is an attitude you choose to embody.** It is a powerful and completely free tool at your disposal, and crucial to your new life in bliss. In fact, it's so crucial that my dear friend, Monte Taylor Jr.,[60] entrepreneur, business coach, and author, has devoted a portion of his book, *Heart Language,* to the topic of gratitude. You can also listen to the lively discussion Monte and I had about the benefits of bliss and gratitude on my website at http://www.practicalbliss.com/blog.

Use the exercise on the next page to begin your gratitude practice.

---

[60]Monte is a serial entrepreneur, coach, business consultant, and the author of the popular marketing blog, "Make Prospecting Easy" at www.montetaylor.com.

EXERCISE - GRATITUDE IS AN ATTITUDE

Step 1: Purchase your journal or find an online version.

Step 2: Find a quiet, comfortable spot to sit.

Step 3: Try playing some soft music to relax or energize you (I relax with Dan Gibson's Piano Cascades).

Step 4: Turn off your phone, email, FB, Twitter, etc., and let your family know you're "on break" for a few minutes and that it's in their best interest to leave you alone! Hint: I tell my son and husband that I promise I'll be much easier to get along with if they grant me these few minutes!

Step 5: Take a moment to just breathe. Nice, slow inhales through your nose, and exhaling through your mouth, two or three times (careful, not too fast—we don't want you hyperventilating!)

Step 6: Current Gratitude List. Think to yourself, if it were your last day on earth, what would you truly give thanks for? Devote the left side of your page to that list.

* **I am currently grateful for (at least four to five items).** Examples: healthy body, friends who care about you, your devoted pets, etc.

Step 7: Gratitude to Be. Close your eyes, suspend your current reality, and imagine yourself in your best life! What does it look and sound like? What are you doing and who are you with? What does it *feel* like to be in this world? Really let yourself be transported and do *not* worry how this will be accomplished. Open your eyes and immediately devote the right side of your page to listing:

***I'm grateful for what's on its way to me (at least four items, written in the present tense).** Examples: You love your work, have plenty of time for self care, rest, relaxation, and personal growth!

It's only in looking back now that I realize that as I was doing this exercise, I began mirroring it with my entire life. In fact, it became a crucial tool for helping me avoid (or surface from) the ever-present threat of depression, which is in my genes and has been known to turn me upside-down without warning in the past. I can't begin to tell you the return on my investment, and I encourage you to use the following exercise to create your own gratitude journal.

EXERCISE - GRATITUDE IS AN ATTITUDE (Bonus)

Bonus Exercise: Think about some of the things for which you have gratitude. What actions did you take in the past to help you achieve those things (i.e, good health, peaceful home, rewarding career, etc.)? What can you learn from your past actions to create your future gratitude?

_____   _____

_____   _____

_____   _____

_____   _____

Potential is Personal

In keeping with my promise to my friend (and myself), I also wrote my thoughts about my "highest self." At the time I really had to suspend my belief as, for the most part, I had allowed my family, friends, and co-workers to define my potential. Looking back, I can now see how incredibly dangerous that practice can be! Letting myself go free of their definitions, I sat quietly, asked God for guidance, and wrote my own take on who I wanted to be.

"I am loving and giving, brilliant and beautiful. I am someone people want to know. My work is excellent, energized, and effective—people seek me out. I'm energized

and fun, funny and I move people to inspiration. People want to hear what I have to say because I am a joyous spirit!

"I'm playful and fun, and sassy and smart and soulful. There is every reason why I am a partner in love. When I speak or counsel, the God inside me comes through me and brings wisdom to my words. I am of God and I cannot forget that or I am denying the gift I have been given. My soul is already aware and my soul WANTS me to have the opportunity to let my message come out! There is NO reason for me to keep to myself. No reason why I cannot or should not have the life I desire. No reason why I shouldn't enjoy every minute, bringing joy and wisdom to everyone!"

I really can't explain where this message of my "higher self" came from. Rereading it, I'm amazed to see a message that I don't even remember thinking or writing, yet I was moved to tears when I read it. I swear sometimes, if we can just get out of our own way, our lives can be so much more meaningful!

As I continued this process over weeks and months (and years), I began to replace the old images and beliefs I had about myself with the new wisdom I found in my freestyle writing. Even better, I began to regularly envision and *feel* the new life that was ahead of me—even in the midst of my current hectic "reality."

The exercise on the next page to begin to envision and step into your "highest self."

EXERCISE - WHO ARE YOU?

As you imagined what your best life is and what's on its way, how did you see yourself? Which of your character strengths can you see (ie, humor, creativity, love of learning, fairness, etc.)? **Who is the "you," the higher self, that wants to be seen? How did you feel as you allowed yourself to imagine?**

Add your thoughts and images here.

Step 8: My highest self is:

Bonus Exercise: Now, and in times of stress or worry, my highest self wants me to know:

Try this exercise more than once, and try not to judge yourself if you don't have a clear picture right away. In the first few months, I recommend practicing steps 1 to 8 every other day (if not every day). As time goes by, you can adjust your frequency to once per week or so. Currently, I practice steps 2 to 4 daily and add in steps 5 to 7 every few weeks or when I need a pick me up or want to capture a particular thought or feeling. I add in step 8 whenever I feel I need to re-center and touch base with who I really am.

In addition to the steps above, I found ways to treat myself to some of the benefits of the blissful life I imagined, without breaking my bank or cramming my schedule. I'd go to the botanical gardens during my lunch, or walk through the Fresh Market grocery store and imagine how I would feel when I could shop there without concern about spending money. To bridge the gap, I'd indulge in a coffee sample, buy little bags of nuts or chocolate, and maybe splurge on a bottle of wine, so that I could even *taste* the bliss that was to be. I also partnered with Dress for Success®, Helen VonDolteren-Fournier[61], and The Ritz Carlton Spa Orlando Grande Lakes on a non-profit project to honor underserved women in the community. This allowed me to give back to others while "working" in a blissful spa environment—what could be better?!

Through the exercises and experiences I've mentioned, I learned that bliss doesn't have to be dependent on something or someone else in order for you to experience it. We can *decide in a moment* to feel bliss any time we want, without waiting for the planets to align and perfection to reveal itself. We can *create the feeling* by exposing ourselves to the thoughts, beliefs, sounds, smells, and tastes of the experiences we long for—any time we decide to. It doesn't mean that we don't have moments of doubt or fear or frustration or mild depression. It simply means that we have more good days than bad by adding more gratitude and joy in, and subtracting the cynicism from our lives. By doing so, we bounce back from disappointments quicker, become alert and ready to welcome bliss when it unexpectedly graces our doorways, and happily work to create moments and memories that make our lives more meaningful.

---

[61] "Law Office of Helen Von Dolteren-Fournier in Winter Park..." 2014, http://www.aegis-rj.com/(accessed April 14, 2016).

CHAPTER EIGHT

Maintaining Your Motivation

"It takes many small shifts to move a mountain."
—Lisa Broesch-Weeks

Are We There Yet?

You know those commercials on TV where there's a dashingly mature man with perfect salt and pepper hair dressed in crisp white pants, a bright polo, and cable knit sweater tied perfectly around his shoulders? Oh, and the slim woman with a beautiful smile and long, flowing hair, looking adoringly up at him while they sail away into the sunset on their yacht? I've always imagined that this was my "someday" life, which would automatically come sailing in around retirement age. I always thought life would be perfect from there on in.

Stop laughing, I'm serious. As ridiculous as it sounds, for years I *truly thought* that this was the "bar" for my bliss, and if I really focused on and dreamt of attaining this destination, I would be all set.

I have what might be startling news. Living in bliss is a journey, much more than a destination. In other words, *it's very possible that you may not really know when you've arrived.*

Where Do You See Evidence of Hope?

I know that if I were sitting in your seat right now I might be asking myself, "What's the point if I don't even know when I've 'made it'?" Another good question—how are you going to truly achieve the bliss we've been talking about if you don't know what that bliss looks like, or what you're shooting for? The simple answer is that creating a life of purpose, engagement, and pleasure is a lot like choosing to take better care of your health through nutrition and exercise. It's a continuous process, not a one-step fix, and you know when you're achieving your goal because you'll notice evidence of hope when you're on track (ie, your clothes are getting looser, you're not out of breath when you walk up a flight of stairs, you feel better, you aren't craving sugar as much as you used to), and when you're off track, you'll notice that, too (ie, clothes are feeling a little snug, you're grazing more, you're not as interested in working out, etc.).

As you look at your overall life now, compared to when you started this process, where do you see evidence that you're reaching your goals? Are you more aware of simple pleasures? Do you invest in more quality time with those you care about? Are you dashing and scurrying less and purposely striding more? Do you find more joy and meaning in your daily life? Do you notice that you're more positive and less negative? Do you experience moments of pure pleasure? In what areas of your life do you see that you've increased your satisfaction?

Exercise – Hope Springs
Use the questions above to answer the following question. Where do you see evidence of hope that you're reaching your

goals and making lasting changes to create more bliss in your life?

_____

_____

_____

_____

Next, look at each area of your life as represented in the Wheel of Life Inventory, and shade in your satisfaction level in *each* area of your life. Note that areas closest to the center indicate lower satisfaction and areas furthest from the center indicate higher satisfaction levels.

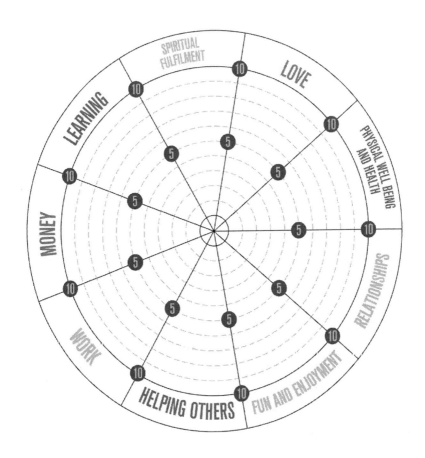

Now, compare your current Wheel of Life Inventory to the one you completed in Chapter 3.

Are you starting to see where you're making progress? Are there areas where you'd like to make more progress? I suspect that the answer to both questions may be "Yes." So let's continue!

At this point we've covered quite a bit of ground:

➢ You now have a clear understanding of bliss in that it isn't an "airy-fairy" nice-to-have thing, but rather a **fundamental factor** in creating a life worth living.

➢ You've also seen how bliss can actually **help you achieve more success** in every area of your life, rather than what most people think bliss will do—distract you from achieving success at work or home.

➢ You've taken a look at how being "self-centered" and self-compassionate **can serve those around you,** because doing both can help you maintain your stamina and build your resilience when you're serving those who depend on you.

➢ You've uncovered (or perhaps reintroduced) your purpose, character strengths, and what brings you passion and flow . . . and have an idea of how you can **practically introduce these elements** to **bring more joy and meaning** into your daily life.

➢ You've taken a look at the optional and mandatory stressors and obligations in your life and how to eliminate and/or manage them where needed so that you can **say "No" where you need to and "Yes" where you want to** and need to!

➢ You've articulated your doubts and fears, to better clarify where you may need to **build strategies and solutions to enable your success** (ie, financial planning, proper insurance, marketing plans, etc.).

➢ You've learned how to shift from a fixed mindset to a growth mindset to **change your outlook and flip failures and obstacles into opportunities** for your success.

➢ You've started to look at more of **what's right in your world**, and choose to have gratitude for the present and future gifts you've been given. Additionally, you've recognized how you've contributed in the past to create some of the things for which you are now grateful.

Excellent work! Now, given all of that, there's still a bit more exploration and work to do before calling it a day.

May the Odds Be Ever In Your Favor!

As I mentioned previously, adding joy and happiness to your life can be your secret weapon against the stress and frustrations that *will* arise around you. As you've no doubt discovered through your own experiences, maintaining a positive lifestyle doesn't mean that you exist in a happy-clappy head-in-the-sand world, but rather a world where the irritations, stress, and pitfalls don't define your existence and can be navigated (and recovered from) more quickly and easily.

When you get into the habit of starting each day with gratitude (yes, even when you're in a hurry, or feeling frustrated, or stuck in traffic, or dealing with pouty kids or spouses or bosses!), and allow yourself to actually *be on the lookout* for internal and external stimulants that bring you peace, hope, joy, laughter, fun, or otherwise blissful emotions, I am willing to bet you will find it. And when you open yourself to really experiencing the emotions, you become more "attract-ive" to others who are looking for the same things. In turn, when you surround yourself with other fun-loving, joy-seeking, successful people, you consciously create a community where you can support and encourage each other in building your In Bliss Life.

A word of caution here: I realize that there's a temptation to sort of mock the idea of a community of fun-loving, joy-seeking people . . . and maybe even look at them as being fanciful dreamers who are off in their own world, enjoying rainbows and unicorns a plenty. In fact, I'm sure the cynical entertainment side of *me* has felt that temptation. I mean seriously, people who *aren't* out to stab you in the back or knock you down in order to build themselves up? Who ever heard of such a thing??! I know, it almost sounds too good to be true. But believe it or not, these people *are* out there, and when you start to open your eyes, seek them out, and reflect that behavior, you'll find those positive people and experiences. Opportunities will appear more and more throughout your life. In fact, you can go to http://www.practicalbliss.com/community to find like-minded future friends right now!

Sneaky Stress Will Find a Way

Armed with your tools, you've definitely stacked the odds in your favor. However, I don't know about you, but I'm constantly amazed at my own ability to create or experience stress at the most unlikely and inopportune of times. Honestly, even when I'm on vacation, stress still finds a way into my life. Here's what I mean . . .

In November of 2006, I attended a retreat in Maui to help me articulate my purpose and create my vision for my soon-to-be-reinvented life. The resort was beautiful and the weather was phenomenal, and as I walked onto the pristine white, shimmering sands of Maui, I couldn't help but marvel at the aquamarine ocean, which seemed to wink at me with each dazzling sparkle of sunshine on its gentle waves. I could barely wait to kick off my shoes and dip my toes into paradise! Within the first five minutes of arrival, I did just that.

I dropped my beach bag and ran with glee to the serene water's edge. As I stepped in, I was happily surprised to see several of my fellow retreat attendees waving and shouting my name from down the beach. I felt so accepted when I saw how joyful they looked, jumping, waving, and frantically calling out to me! At this point, their shouts seemed like overkill, but I appreciated it just the same. Until I focused on their cries and realized that they were actually shouting for me to **GET OUT OF THE WATER!** Startled by the aggressive warning, I jumped back immediately, just in time to see a five-foot *killer* shark skim through the ankle-deep water within two feet of where I now stood on the sand!

As I jumped backwards into the sand, narrowly avoiding certain death, my right heel landed squarely on a bumblebee that promptly (and rudely!) stung me in the process. Seriously?? A bumblebee on the beach? Certainly a hazard I had never anticipated.

Yes, stress finds a way.

Having just survived the ordeal, I began to get caught up in the fear and pain that I encountered in those brief moments. I told the story to everyone I met, reveling in my unexpected drama and misfortune in paradise. The whole thing was quite dramatic.

Fortunately, I shortly thereafter caught myself in the act of complaining and realized that sometimes stress just finds a way, and in those times we need to be prepared to be as flexible and resilient as we can possibly be so that we recover within a few short moments rather than days, weeks, or longer.

This is why it's so important for us to eliminate the optional stress, prepare strategies for the mandatory stress and obligations, and focus on what's going well rather than honing in on what went differently than you expected.

So when those moments come up, laugh about them if you can! I know that not every stressor is going to be something you can find funny at the time, but some of those moments might be worthy of a chuckle once you've survived them. In fact, I used the story of my trouble in paradise as the opening to a speech I gave to women attending my Stress to Success program in an Orlando convention,[62] and they certainly got a laugh out of it!

A dear friend of mine, Mary, told me the story of how she lost her brand new Prada backpack, which contained her camera, all of her vacation photos, and assorted medications, in a taxi while visiting family in Italy. At the time she was more than stressed, but the story she tells of her family searching for the backpack and scrambling to recreate the photos and replace the medications is hysterical. And now whenever anyone mentions Italy, I can't help but think of the Prada backpack adventure and laugh.

The Power of HQCs (High Quality Connections)

"The worst solitude is to have no real friendships." —Francis Bacon

Speaking of laughter and friends, I really can't stress enough how important it is to have at least one healthy, positive relationship in your life, and now that you're on your way to finding bliss, this will become even more important. It could be a friend, spouse, sibling, coworker, or otherwise. Trust your instincts; when you're in a positive relationship where you feel happy, healthy, energized, inspired, validated, authentic, and respected, you'll feel good when you're around that person (or those people). And that means that's the

---

[62] Email me at Lisa@PracticalBliss.com for a complimentary copy of the Stress to Success DVD

person to lean on and stick close to when you're aspiring toward bliss.

Researchers Stephens, Heaphy, and Dutton call these "High Quality Connections,"[63] (HQC) and note that these relationships are also based on a mutual admiration for each other's best interest, and are positive and even playful at times.

The researchers go on to say that having an HQC at work has been linked to having a greater intention to stay at a particular job, which would make sense since you would feel a sense of belonging. Additionally, even small amounts of positive interaction can increase speed and memory at work, according to additional studies.[64] And when members of a team have high-quality connections, they may also feel more safety and trust, resulting in greater cooperation and coordination.

On the flip side, when you're in an unhealthy or lopsided friendship that creates feelings of being manipulated, insulted, disrespected, undervalued, stressed out, or just plain feels bad, you'll know that, too, and you'll know how it's affecting you in your own journey. You'll feel it in your body, and may even experience headaches, body aches, or a feeling of exhaustion while you're with the person (or immediately afterwards). If this rings a bell, it means it's time to stop making excuses for why you're in this relationship and eliminate or severely limit your time with that person, to the best of your ability.

---

[63] Stephens, J.P., Heaphy, E., & Dutton, J.E. *High-quality Connections.* The Oxford Handbook of Positive Organizational Scholarship, 29, 385. New York: Oxford University Press, 2012.
[64] Ybarra, O., Burnstein, E., Winkielman, P., Keller, M.C., Manis, M., Chan, E., & Rodriguez, J. Mental exercising through simple socializing: Social interaction promotes general cognitive functioning. *Personality and Social Psychology Bulletin,* 34(2) (2008), 248-259.

All that is to say, when you establish a true BFF, you're likely to experience more joy, energy, meaning, connection, fun, and acceptance in both your personal and professional worlds—which can only help you in your search for bliss.

So if you haven't already done so, it may be time to devote a little energy to assessing the relationships you have in your life, to ensure that you have at least one friendship that meets the HQC standards.

EXERCISE – WHO ARE YOUR H.Q.C.s (High Quality Connections)?

Review the information below to assess your personal and professional relationships.

On the lines below, list the people with whom you are in relationship (personally and professionally). Use the prompts below to code your list and discover your HQC relationships.

_____   _____   _____

_____   _____   _____

Next, reviewing your list, place a * next to the relationships that are positive, authentic, reliable, respectful, and credible. **Example:**

Kim*	Beth	Terry*
Kevin*	Mary*	Eileen

Now place a + next to those with whom your relationship contains mutual regard for each other's best interests, empathy, positive emotions and perhaps even play. **Example:**

Kim*+	Beth	Terry*
Kevin*+	Mary*+	Eileen

Circle each relationship that meets the criteria above and makes you feel energized (rather than drained), connected and accepted. **Example:**

(Kim*+)	Beth	Terry*
(Kevin*+)	(Mary*+)	Eileen

Lastly, strike through any relationships that drain you, don't feel positive, or aren't based on authenticity, reliability, and respect. Note, this doesn't mean that you need to terminate the relationship (especially if you're talking about a family member). It just means you are aware that these relationships are not of the high quality standard. **Example:**

(Kim*+)	~~Beth~~	Terry*
(Kevin*+)	(Mary*+)	~~Eileen~~

All relationships that contain * + and a circle are likely your highest quality relationships!

(Kim*+)   (Kevin*+)   (Mary*+)

If you find that you have at least one HQC (could be your spouse, significant other, peer at work, neighbor, long-time friend, or other), that's great—move on to the next step! If not, it looks like you may want to invest some time in finding ways to meet people who are looking for similar qualities in a relationship. Emotions are contagious, and it's important that you're surrounding yourself with people who display the kinds of traits and energy you want to "catch."

Not sure where to find them? For me, I've found some of my closest, highest-quality friendships while attending workshops and retreats (some have been only one- or two-day events), through friends of my closest friends, and through my husband's friends. You can also check out the www.theflourishingcenter.com, where people who are interested in positive psychology gather, your local optimist clubs, www.meetup.com, or connect with them through other social media. Of course, you can also get involved in Club Bliss and other great communities—there are plenty of opportunities out there, so go find them!

Once you've established those relationships, make sure you're doing everything you can to foster them! This doesn't need to take hours or longer; in fact, you can just take a few moments here and there (when it's convenient for you) to check in if you haven't connected in a while. Ask them to share what's going on in their world—ask how their health is, what are they doing for fun, whether they are taking care of themselves, and anything else you'd like a friend to know about you. Of course, you don't want to force these questions onto someone you've only known for two weeks. Obviously trust doesn't happen overnight, and you don't want to give off a stalker vibe!

I can honestly say that over the last decade I've been acutely aware of the quality of friendships I foster and maintain in my life, and I've worked to eliminate or minimize contact with the relationships in which I feel drained, diminished, frustrated, or stressed out. Additionally, I encourage my friends to be friends with each other, because there really is no limit to the amount of positive influence you allow into your life, and the benefits far outweigh your minimal investment of time and energy.

Don't Hate the Haters

So now we've worked toward building your bliss for yourself, and finding ways to incorporate the right people into your life. We've figured out who is helping and who is hurting, and what to do about that. And at this point in our relationship, I feel I can share a little something I've learned over the years so that you can avoid taking it personally when you encounter this anomaly.

Sooner or later, all this bliss and joy and happiness business—all the things you've worked so hard for throughout the book, and are going to keep working for—is going to tick someone off. Yup, I know, seems ridiculous right?

I know because it's happened to me a few times, and it usually seems to come out of nowhere. You'll be happily going about your day, minding your own business, perhaps even smiling at people on the street . . . and then **BAM!** Someone you may or may not personally know decides to tell you how they feel about your happy self, just because they feel they should. It doesn't really seem to make any sense, and it can actually sting worse than a bee. It may even leave you reeling for days, if not longer.

There's a reason for that. When you choose to live your life in a positive and joyful way, you're breathing rarified air. It just isn't the "norm," and for some reason that irritates the heck out of some people. It could be that they've never encountered the kind of happiness and meaning in their lives that you now radiate, and they may think the whole thing is just for "show." They may also feel resentment toward you because you appear to be happy when they're far from achieving honest-to-goodness happiness. Some may even feel that your positivity and lifestyle illuminate the negative world in which they may live and have been unsuccessfully trying to ignore.

The best advice I can offer is to stay your course, even when the temptation to bite back at these people may be so strong that you can hardly hold it at bay. Smile gracefully, explain your point of view if you feel it's the right time and place, and wish them all the best. The energy suck that can come as a result of engaging in petty altercations isn't something I choose to give way to, and I'm guessing you won't enjoy it either. Now that you've found your bliss, enjoy it for all it's worth. And don't allow others to pull you out of it.

When Conflicts Occur

That being said, I've no doubt that you're like most humans in that there are people in this world who have used words, actions, or behaviors that have hurt you deeply. I get it, I really do—and that's how I know how much those open wounds can get in the way of obtaining true bliss.

That's why it's important to take a look at your Wheel of Life Inventory to see whether you want to somehow close the loop on some outstanding relationship, life, or work issues. Is there something in your life that's taking up more energy than it should, or giving you a negative experience? Is that keeping you from moving forward and truly finding your bliss?

I'm not suggesting that you have to go back to each person and tell them you forgive them, though studies have shown[65] that forgiveness will help *you* release hatred and troubled feelings and allow you to experience more serenity than those who hang on to the conflict. As a matter of fact, forgiveness can also do wonders when you're feeling hateful, depressed, or anxious.

Keep in mind that forgiving someone doesn't mean you need to forget what's occurred (especially if you've learned a valuable lesson or justice hasn't been served). It simply means you're not going to carry those damaging emotions anymore, even if you decide to forgive those people without personally letting them know that you've done so. This is another aspect of cutting the negativity from your life so that you can move forward into bliss. It doesn't always mean cutting negative people from your life (sometimes that's just not possible), but it does mean getting rid of the negative emotions that are holding you back. Make sense?

Can you think of anyone you need to forgive in order to help claim your inner bliss? If so, you can find additional information on how to practice forgiveness by visiting Colin Tipping's website[66]. Be sure you also include forgiving yourself for mistakes you've made or things you've done wrong to yourself or others. You can start by applying a practice of self-compassion, as you read about earlier in this book.

Noticing the Not So Obvious

---

[65] Peterson, C. *A Primer in Positive Psychology.* New York: Oxford University Press, 2007.
[66] www.radicalforgiveness.com

As we approach the end of this phase of our journey together, how are you feeling (physically and mentally)? Are you starting to feel a little lighter and happier?

If by chance you aren't, I invite you try a few additional interventions that may work for you, as they have for me.

First, if you're feeling that you just can't shake those feelings of being overwhelmed, anxious, depressed, or fatigued, you may want to see a doctor. Not just any doctor, but one who will run a full diagnostic inquiry through lab work and examination to ensure that you're not dealing with a chemical, hormone, or other such imbalance.

For me, I encountered a brief period of time a few years ago where I fell into a cycle of exhaustion that led to anxiety and ultimately mild depression. I must have seen two or three doctors before I found one who ran a battery of tests and asked many questions before discovering that I had both a thyroid and testosterone imbalance. As I followed my doctor's advice on how to correct the imbalance, I also worked to bring in more exercise and other things I enjoyed, to boost my feelings of success.

Additionally, Dr. Daniel Thomas,[67] an anti-aging physician with over twenty-five years of experience, recommends (in addition to proper medication) a healthy diet, spending time in nature, and connecting with positive people to combat depression and anxiety and increase positive emotions.

Leslie Davis,[68] a thriving health coach, agrees, and reminds us to consider the link between how we feel about ourselves physically and our emotional state:

---

[67]Dr. Daniel Thomas, anti-aging physician, with over twenty-five years of experience www.HealthyandStrong.com.
[68]Leslie Davis is founder and CEO of www.FITSSIMPLE.com. She's a certified fitness instructor and a top Team Beachbody coach.

The way you feel about yourself and your surroundings can be impacted by how you feel physically . . . bliss has an impact on reaching your overall health goals; when you're truly taking care of yourself and maintaining your emotional needs as well as your physical, you can avoid using food as a source of comfort, which in turn helps you achieve the healthy and fit body you desire. When you don't you may use food as an artificial bliss and get the opposite effect. When you align both - one contributes to the other.

If you find that despite your efforts, you can't seem to shake a physical roadblock to your success, make sure you include professional advice as I did. The great thing is, every step in the process that we've discussed in this guide can be done *in combination with* most medical interventions to help you reach your goals. Nothing should hold you back from achieving bliss.

One More Out the Door

So let's say you've followed every bit of advice and completed every exercise I've offered and yet you aren't reaching your goals as quickly or effectively as you would have liked. Ugh—I can only imagine how frustrating that must feel! But here are a few additional elements I'd like you to consider as you're reviewing your progress.

First, keep in mind that changes don't happen all at once, even if you really *really* want them to. It truly is small shifts that move a mountain, and sometimes those shifts are so small that you wouldn't notice them even if you were standing on the mountain looking for them!

It may be possible that you need to look at your goals and break them down into micro projects that are more easily measurable and achievable. You may also want to ensure that you're *consistently* working toward your goals (rather than occasionally introducing a burst of time and energy). To do so, try approaching your calendar quite differently than you've likely done it in the past. By that, I mean look at the next two, three, or four weeks on your calendar and block out time to invest in your bliss (before you schedule other things). Then let your other responsibilities revolve around those "Bliss Blocks" of time.

Examples of investing in bliss can be exercise, hobbies, practicing mindfulness, being in nature, getting together with your HQC, trying new recipes, and doing any of the things that bring you flow—as we identified earlier.

How to Book Your Bliss Blocks

Take a look at my sample calendar, on the next page. Notice that I code all Bliss Blocks in their own color to remind myself to protect them!

EXAMPLE:

TIME	MONDAY	TUESDAY	WEDS	THURS	FRIDAY	SATURDAY	SUNDAY
8a		Mini meditaion before work				Mini meditataion	
9a						Painting class!	
10a							
11a							
12p		Take a walk/eat lunch outside					
1p							
2p							
3p							
4p			15 min Power walk		Work on computer projects outside		Me time! Reading in hammock!
5p							
6p				Yoga Class!		Dinner with BFF/Spouse	
7p							Play with my kids!

The key is to protect those blocks of time as you would protect the blocks you have scheduled for other important things in your life. When things come up that are mandatory, and upend your plans, be sure to reschedule your Bliss Block for the next available time/day.

Exercise – Booking Your Bliss Blocks

Take a look at your schedule for the next couple of weeks. Set aside Bliss Blocks on your schedule to do things that help you achieve purpose, engagement, and pleasure (bliss) in your life.

Looking For Bits of Bliss?

When it comes to quickly thinking of ways to bring more Bits of Bliss into your life, I realize that it can be tricky to switch from the left-brain mentality associated with everyday challenges and to-do lists to the right-brained mentality associated with keeping quick bliss ideas at your fingertips. For this reason, I've listed a few low-cost, low-effort ideas to spark your creativity.

—**Smile!** When it comes to creating feelings of happiness, nothing works quicker than putting an honest-to-goodness smile on your face. Smiling helps to boost your immune system, reduce stress, lower blood pressure, and radiate and attract positive energy—which then works to further improve your feelings of positivity.

—**Bring the outdoors in!** Ever notice how flowers can brighten your day? You're not alone. Studies show that bringing plants indoors can actually improve both task performance and mood, especially in men.[69] So on your next trip to the store, be sure to pick up a little greenery to brighten up your home and office.

—**Take a walk.** Walking will not only contribute to your health and fitness, but also helps to improve your overall outlook and perspective. Want to double your benefits? Invite others to walk with you, and challenge each other to point out all of the elements you encounter on your route that bring you bliss.

—**Lighten up!** Open up those blinds, sit in the sun, invest in a light energy lamp (often used to treat Seasonal Affective Disorder)—do whatever it takes to shine a light on your life.

---

[69] "Effects of the foliage plant on task performance and mood," 2012, http://www.academia.edu/574012/Effects_of_the_foliage_plant_on_task_performance_and_mood (accessed April 14, 2016).

Studies show that increasing your light exposure is related to improved quality of life and social and emotional functioning.[70]

—**Reach out and touch someone.** I know that when I hear from a friend who has shared that they just went through a "tough time," my first response is *"Why didn't you call me?!"* Sometimes our instincts tell us to hunker down and ride out the storm solo, when the best cure for a temporary situation may be the laughter and wisdom of a close friend.

—**Treat yourself.** Dining alone? Why not pull out the good dishes, silverware, and glasses (I'll even drink my water out of a wine glass to make it even more fun) normally reserved for company? I'm guessing you bought those place settings because you liked them, so why not enjoy them all the time?

—**Move your body!!** We hear so much about how we *should* work out to improve our health, but did you know that activity can also boost our mood and lower rates of depression? Some activity is better than none, so don't wait until the conditions are perfect to start an exercise plan. Get up and go!

—**Keep a "Bliss Book."** Try keeping a small notebook with you, and jot down anything that brings you joy, peace, happiness, love, energy, passion, or great memories. Adding to the list will keep you focused on what matters to you, and reviewing it will help boost your mood when you need a pick-me-up.

—**Slow your roll**. Whenever you find yourself scurrying and dashing to your next "thing," take a moment to slow down, take longer strides, hold your head up high, and bre-ee-athe slowly and deeply. You'll arrive at your destination at roughly the same time and you'll feel more calm, cool, and collected in the process.

---

[70] Grandner, Michael A., Daniel F. Kripke, and Robert D. Langer. "Light exposure is related to social and emotional functioning and to quality of life in older women." *Psychiatry Research* 143.1 (2006): 35-42.

—**Keep a list of what's going right**—and refer to it often!

—**Create the soundtrack for your life.** Start, end, or anywhere in between, keep your favorite feel-good music on your phone or other device so you can access it easily and give yourself a pick-me-up when you need it most.

—**Bliss By the Road**—Does your career keep you on the road? I feel your pain! I currently divide my time between homes in two states and frequently travel when speaking or consulting. Check out http://inblisslife.com/bliss/bliss-by-the-road/h to gain tips to make your travel less tedious.

-- **Bliss Gone Bad**—Let's face it, sometimes our best bliss efforts go bad! Share your moments and read stories from others at http://inblisslife.com/bliss/bliss-gone-bad/

Looking for more Bits of Bliss™? Go to http://inblisslife.com/bliss/bits-of-bliss/ for tips to keep your momentum going and to share *your* Bits of Bliss™ with our community!

Bliss Is an Ongoing Experience—Not a Final Destination

As you continue on your path to a life filled with purpose, engagement, and pleasure, remember that this is an ongoing journey that doesn't end when you reach the last page of this guide. Not by a long shot. This is your new way of life! I fully encourage you to go to PracticalBliss.com or email Lisa@PracticalBliss.com to connect with me, share feedback about your journey using this guide, gain additional tips and tools, listen to interviews with some of the experts who contributed to this guide, find out about upcoming retreats and workshops, and even claim your complimentary coaching session!

As you've completed the steps here, celebrate your success! It's so important to make sure you find ways to really celebrate what you're doing to take charge of your own happiness! You are the only one who is really and truly going to make this happen. You don't need to wait until your life is smooth sailing (remember, a lot of the tools in this guide will actually work to help you gain more control over your life!) or you gain buy-in from anyone else. You'll never again be as young as you are in this moment, and there's not a moment to waste!!

May you work, play, live . . . InBliss!™

Blissful Bits to Remember . . .

Blissful Bits to Remember . . .

Blissful Bits to Remember . . .

Get More Great Stuff

Download All the Exercises In This Book!!
Just go to www.Practicalbliss.com/resources/bonus

Request Your Complimentary
Coaching Session
Just go to http://inblisslife.com/30-minute-consultation/

Join the Next Happiness Retreat!
Go to http://inblisslife.com/coaching/retreats/
for dates and details.

Claim Your Complimentary BONUS Video:
Stress to Success!

The video contains content not included in this book that will
help you create a Life In Bliss! Just contact me through my
website: http://www.Practicalbliss.com/contact and request
your complimentary copy.

Do you have stories of "Bliss Gone Bad" or "Bits of Bliss" you'd like
to share? I'd love to hear from you and may even feature your story
in our Club Bliss Community!

Made in the USA
Lexington, KY
04 July 2016